LOW-FAT COOKING

DISHES FOR DELICIOUSLY NUTRITIOUS
HEALTHY EATING

Consultant Editor: Anne Sheasby

HERMES
HOUSE

Published in 2000 by Hermes House

© Anness Publishing Limited 2000

Hermes House is an imprint of
Anness Publishing Limited
Hermes House, 88-89 Blackfriars Road
London SE1 8HA

A CIP catalogue record for this book is available from the British Library

Publisher: Joanna Lorenz
Senior Editor: Linda Fraser
Designer: Sara Kidd
Photographers: Karl Adamson, Steve Baxter, Amanda Heywood. Michael Michaels, Don Last,
Edward Allwright, Thomas Odulate, James Duncan, Peter Reilly, Patrick McLeavey
Recipes: Carla Capalbo and Laura Washburn, Stephen Wheeler, Christine France, Shirley Gill, Roz
Denny, Annie Nichols, Linda Fraser, Catherine Atkinson, Maggie Pannell,
Kit Chan, Sue Maggs, Christine Ingram
Home Economists: Wendy Lee, Jane Stevenson, Elizabeth Wolf Cohen,
Kit Chan assisted by Lucy McKelvie, Kathryn Hawkins
Stylists: Blake Minton and Kirsty Rawlings, Fiona Tillett, Hilary Guy, Thomas Odulate,
Madeleine Brehaut, Jo Harris

Previously published as part of a larger compendium, *The Ultimate Fat Free Cookbook*

Printed in Hong Kong/China

1 3 5 7 9 10 8 6 4 2

NOTES
For all recipes, quantities are given in both metric and imperial measures and, where appropriate,
measures are also given in standard cups and spoons. Follow one set but not a mixture because they
are not interchangeable.

Standard spoon and cup measures are level.
1 tsp = 5ml, 1 tbsp = 15ml, 1 cup = 8fl oz/250ml.

Medium eggs should be used unless otherwise stated.

LOW
COOKING

Contents

Introduction

A healthy diet is one that provides the body with all the nutrients it needs to be able to grow and repair properly. By eating the right types, balance and proportions of foods, we are more likely to feel healthy, have plenty of energy and a higher resistance to illness that will help protect our body against developing diseases such as heart disease, cancers, bowel disorders and obesity.

By choosing a variety of foods every day, you will ensure that you are supplying your body with all the essential nutrients, including vitamins and minerals, it needs. To get the balance right, it is important to know just how much of each type of food you should be eating.

There are five main food groups (see right), and it is recommended that we should eat plenty of fruit, vegetables (at least five portions a day, not including potatoes) and foods such as cereals,

pasta, rice and potatoes; moderate amounts of meat, fish, poultry and dairy products; and only small amounts of foods containing fat or sugar. By choosing a good balance of foods from these groups every day, and choosing lower fat or lower sugar alternatives wherever possible, we will be supplying our bodies with all the nutrients they need for optimum health.

THE ROLE AND IMPORTANCE OF FAT IN OUR DIET

Fats shouldn't be cut out of our diets completely. We need a small amount of fat for general health and well-being – fat is a valuable source of energy, and also helps to make foods more palatable to eat. However, if you lower the fats, especially saturated fats, in your diet, you will feel healthier; it will help you lose weight and reduce the risk of developing some diseases.

THE FIVE MAIN FOOD GROUPS

● Fruit and vegetables

● Rice, potatoes, bread, pasta and other cereals

● Meat, poultry, fish and alternative proteins

● Milk and other dairy foods

● Foods which contain fat and foods which contain sugar

Aim to limit your daily intake of fats to no more than 30% of total calories. In real terms, this means that for an average intake of 2,000 calories per day, 30% of energy would come from 600 calories. Since each gram of fat provides 9 calories, your total daily intake should be no more than 66.6g fat. Your total intake of saturated fats should be no more than 10% of the total calories.

TYPES OF FAT

All fats in our foods are made up of building blocks of fatty acids and glycerol and their properties vary according to each combination.

There are two types of fat – saturated and unsaturated. The unsaturated group is divided into two types – polyunsaturated and monounsaturated fats.

There is always a combination of each of the three types of fat (saturated, polyunsaturated and monounsaturated fats) in any food, but the amount of each type varies greatly from one food to another.

Left: By choosing a variety of foods from the five main food groups, you will ensure that you are supplying your body with all the nutrients it needs.

SATURATED FATS

All fatty acids are made up of chains of carbon atoms. Each atom has one or more free "bonds" to link with other atoms and by doing so the fatty acids transport nutrients to cells throughout the body. Without these free "bonds" the atom cannot form any links, that is to say it is completely "saturated". Because of this, the body finds it hard to process the fatty acid into energy, so it simply stores it as fat.

Saturated fats are the fats which you should reduce, as they can increase the level of cholesterol in the blood, which in turn can increase the risk of developing heart disease.

The main sources of saturated fats are animal products, such as meat, and fats, such as butter and lard that are solid at room temperature. However, there are also saturated fats of vegetable origin, notably coconut and palm oils, and some margarines and oils, which are processed by changing some of the unsaturated fatty acids to saturated ones – they are labelled "hydrogenated vegetable oil" and should be avoided.

POLYUNSATURATED FATS

There are two types of polyunsaturated fats, those of vegetable or plant origin (omega 6), such as sunflower oil, soft margarine and seeds, and those from oily fish (omega 3), such as herring, mackerel and sardines. Both fats are usually liquid at room temperature. Small quantities of polyunsaturated fats are essential for good health and are thought to help reduce the level of cholesterol in the blood.

MONOUNSATURATED FATS

Monounsaturated fats are also thought to have the beneficial effect of reducing the blood cholesterol level and this could explain why in some

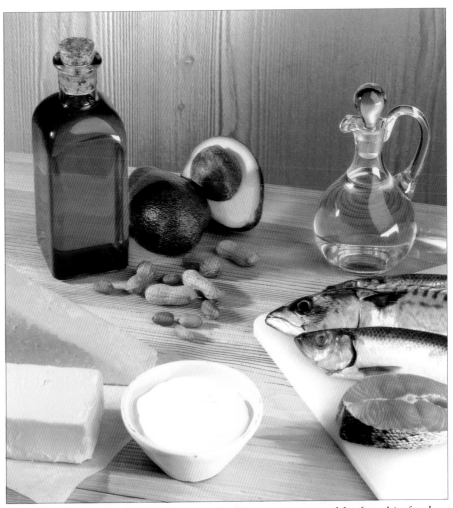

Above: A selection of foods containing the three main types of fat found in foods.

Mediterranean countries there is such a low incidence of heart disease. Monounsaturated fats are found in foods such as olive oil, rapeseed oil, some nuts such as almonds and hazel-nuts, oily fish and avocado pears.

CUTTING DOWN ON FATS AND SATURATED FATS IN THE DIET

About one quarter of the fat we eat comes from meat and meat products, one-fifth from dairy products and margarine and the rest from cakes, biscuits, pastries and other foods. It is easy to cut down on obvious sources of fat in the diet, such as butter, oils, margarine, cream, whole milk and full fat cheese, but we also need to know

about – and watch out for – "hidden" fats. Hidden fats can be found in foods such as cakes, biscuits and nuts. Even lean, trimmed red meats may contain as much as 10% fat.

By being aware of foods which are high in fats and particularly saturated fats, and by making simple changes to your diet, you can reduce the total fat content of your diet quite considerably. Whenever possible, choose reduced fat or low fat alternatives to foods such as milk, cheese and salad dressings, and fill up on very low fat foods, such as fruit and vegetables, and foods that are high in carbohydrate such as pasta, rice, bread and potatoes.

EASY WAYS TO CUT DOWN FAT AND SATURATED FAT IN THE DAILY DIET

There are lots of simple no-fuss ways of reducing the fat in your diet. Just follow the simple "eat less – try instead" suggestions below to discover how easy it is.

● EAT LESS – Butter, margarine and hard fats.
● TRY INSTEAD – Low fat spread, very low fat spread or polyunsaturated margarine. If you must use butter or hard margarine, make sure they are softened at room temperature and spread them very thinly. Better still, use fat-free spreads such as low fat soft cheese, reduced sugar jams or marmalades for sandwiches and toast.

● EAT LESS – Fatty meats and high fat products such as meat pâtés, pies and sausages.
● TRY INSTEAD – Low fat meats, such as chicken, turkey and venison.
   Use only the leanest cuts of such meats as lamb, beef and pork.
   Always cut any visible fat and skin from meat before cooking.
   Choose reduced fat sausages and meat products and eat fish more often.
   Try using low fat protein products such as Quorn or tofu in place of meat in recipes.
   Make gravies using vegetable water or fat-free stock rather than using meat juices.

● EAT LESS – Full fat dairy products such as whole milk, cream, butter, hard margarine, crème fraîche, whole milk yogurts and hard cheese.
● TRY INSTEAD – Semi-skimmed or skimmed milk and milk products, low fat yogurts, low fat fromage frais and low fat soft cheeses, reduced fat hard cheeses such as Cheddar, and reduced fat creams and crème fraîche.

● EAT LESS – Hard cooking fats, such as lard or hard margarine.
● TRY INSTEAD – Polyunsaturated or monounsaturated oils, such as olive, sunflower or corn for cooking.

● EAT LESS – Rich salad dressings like full-fat mayonnaise, salad cream or French dressing.
● TRY INSTEAD – Reduced fat or fat-free mayonnaise or dressings. Make salad dressings at home with low fat yogurt or fromage frais.

● EAT LESS – Fried foods.
● TRY INSTEAD – Fat-free cooking methods such as grilling, microwaving, steaming or baking whenever possible.
   Try cooking in a non-stick wok with only a very small amount of oil.
   Always roast or grill meat or poultry on a rack.

● EAT LESS – Deep-fried chips and sautéed potatoes.
● TRY INSTEAD – Fat-free starchy foods such as pasta, couscous and rice.
   Choose baked or boiled potatoes.

● EAT LESS – Added fat in cooking.
● TRY INSTEAD – To cook with little or no fat. Use heavy-based or good quality non-stick pans, so that the food doesn't stick.
   Try using a small amount of spray oil in cooking to control exactly how much fat you are using.
   Use fat-free or low fat ingredients for cooking, such as fruit juice, low fat or fat-free stock, wine or even beer.

● EAT LESS – High fat snacks such as crisps, tortilla chips, fried snacks and pastries, chocolate cakes, muffins, doughnuts, sweet pastries and biscuits – especially chocolate ones!
● TRY INSTEAD – Low fat and fat-free fresh or dried fruits, breadsticks or vegetable sticks.
   Make your own home-baked low fat cakes and bakes.
   If you do buy ready-made cakes and biscuits, always choose low fat and reduced fat versions.

FAT-FREE COOKING METHODS

It's very easy to cook without fat – whenever possible, grill, bake, microwave or steam foods without the addition of fat, or try stir-frying without fat – use a little low fat or fat-free stock, wine or fruit juice instead.

● Choosing heavy-based or good quality cookware, you'll find that the amount of fat needed for cooking foods can be kept to an absolute minimum. When making casseroles or meat sauces such as bolognese, dry-fry the meat to brown it and then drain off all the excess fat before adding the other ingredients. If you do need a little fat for cooking, choose an oil which is high in unsaturates such as corn, sunflower, olive or rapeseed oil and always use as little as possible.

● When baking low fat cakes and bakes, use good quality bakeware which doesn't need greasing before use, or use non-stick baking paper and only lightly grease before lining.

● Look out for non-stick coated fabric sheet. This re-usable non-stick material is amazingly versatile, it can be cut to size and used to line cake tins, baking sheets or frying pans. Heat resistant up to 290°C/550°F and microwave safe, it will last for up to 5 years.

● When baking foods such as chicken or fish, rather than adding a knob of butter to the food, try baking the food in a loosely sealed parcel of foil or greaseproof paper and adding some wine or fruit juice and herbs or spices to the food before sealing the parcel.

● When grilling foods, the addition of fat is often unnecessary. If the food shows signs of drying, lightly brush with a small amount of unsaturated oil such as sunflower or corn oil.

Above: Invest in a few of these useful items of cookware for easy fat-free cooking: non-stick cookware and accurate measuring equipment are essential.

● Microwaved foods rarely need the addition of fat, so add herbs or spices for extra flavour and colour.

● Steaming or boiling are easy, fat-free ways of cooking many foods, especially vegetables, fish and chicken.

● Try poaching foods, such as chicken, fish and fruit, in stock or syrup – it is another easy, fat-free cooking method.

● Try braising vegetables in the oven in low fat or fat-free stock, wine or simply water with the addition of some herbs.

● Sauté vegetables in low fat or fat-free stock, wine or fruit juice instead of fat or oil.

● Cook vegetables in a covered saucepan over a low heat with a little water so they cook in their own juices.

● Marinate food such as meat or poultry in mixtures of alcohol, herbs or spices, and vinegar or fruit juice. This will help to tenderize the meat and add flavour and colour and, in addition, the marinade can be used to baste the food while it is cooking.

● When serving vegetables such as boiled potatoes, carrots or peas, resist the temptation to add a knob of butter or margarine. Instead, sprinkle with chopped fresh herbs or ground spices.

COOKING WITH LOW FAT OR NON-FAT INGREDIENTS

Nowadays many foods are available in full fat and reduced fat or very low fat forms. In every supermarket you'll find a huge array of low fat dairy products, such as milk, cream, yogurt, hard and soft cheeses and fromage frais; reduced fat sweet or chocolate biscuits; reduced fat or fat-free salad dressings and mayonnaise; reduced fat crisps and snacks; low fat, half-fat or very low fat spreads; as well as such reduced fat ready-made food products as desserts.

Other foods, such as fresh fruit and vegetables, pasta, rice, potatoes and bread, naturally contain very little fat. Some foods, such as soy sauce, wine, cider, sherry, sugar, honey, syrup and jam, contain no fat at all. By combining these and other low fat foods you can create delicious dishes which contain very little fat.

Some low fat or reduced fat ingredients and products work better than others in cooking but often a simple substitution of one for another will work. The addition of low fat or non-fat ingredients, such as herbs and spices, also add plenty of extra flavour and colour to recipes.

LOW FAT SPREADS IN COOKING

There is a huge variety of low fat, reduced fat and half-fat spreads available in our supermarkets, along with some spreads that are very low in fat. Some are suitable for cooking, while others are only suitable for spreading.

Generally speaking, the very low fat spreads with a fat content of around 20% or less have a high water content and so are all unsuitable for cooking and are only suitable for spreading.

Low fat or half-fat spreads with a fat content of around 40% are suitable for spreading and can be used for some cooking methods. They are suitable for recipes such as all-in-one cake and biscuit recipes, all-in-one sauce recipes, sautéing vegetables over a low heat, choux pastry and some cake icings.

When using these low fat spreads for cooking, the fat may behave slightly differently to full fat products such as butter or margarine.

With some recipes, the cooked result may be slightly different, but will still be very acceptable. Other recipes will be just as tasty and successful. For example, choux pastry made using half- or low fat spread is often slightly crisper and lighter in texture than traditional choux pastry, and a cheesecake biscuit base made with melted half- or low fat spread combined with crushed biscuit crumbs, may be slightly softer in texture and less crispy than a biscuit base made using melted butter.

When heating half- or low fat spreads, never cook them over a high heat. Always use a heavy-based pan over a low heat to avoid the product burning, spitting or spoiling, and stir all the time. With all-in-one sauces, the mixture should be whisked continuously over a low heat.

Half-fat or low fat spreads are not suitable for shallow or deep-fat frying, pastry making, rich fruit cakes, some biscuits, shortbread, clarified butter and preserves such as lemon curd.

Remember that the keeping qualities of recipes made using half- or low fat spreads may be reduced slightly, due to the lower fat content.

Almost all dairy products now come in low fat or reduced fat versions.

Another way to reduce the fat content of recipes, particularly cake recipes is to use a fruit purée in place of all or some of the fat in a recipe.

Many cake recipes work well using this method but others may not be so successful. Pastry does not work well. Breads work very well, perhaps because the amount of fat is usually relatively small, as do some biscuits and bars, such as brownies and flapjacks.

To make the dried fruit purée to use in recipes, chop 115g/4oz ready-to-eat dried fruit and place in a blender or food processor with 75ml/5 tbsp water and blend to a roughly smooth purée. Then, simply substitute the same weight of this dried fruit purée for all or just some of the amount of fat in the recipe. The purée will keep in the fridge for up to three days.

You can use prunes, dried apricots, dried peaches, or dried apples, or substitute mashed fresh fruit, such as ripe bananas or lightly cooked apples, without the added water.

Above: A selection of cooking oils and low fat spreads. Always check the packaging of low fat spreads – for cooking, they must have a fat content of about 40%.

LOW FAT AND VERY LOW FAT SNACKS

Instead of reaching for a packet of crisps, a high fat biscuit or a chocolate bar when hunger strikes, choose one of these tasty low fat snacks to fill that hungry hole.

● A piece of fresh fruit or vegetable such as an apple, banana or carrot – keep chunks or sticks wrapped in a polythene bag in the fridge.

● Fresh fruit or vegetable chunks – skewer them on to cocktail sticks or short bamboo skewers to make them into mini kebabs.

● A handful of dried fruit such as raisins, apricots or sultanas. These also make a perfect addition to children's packed lunches or to school break snacks.

● A portion of canned fruit in natural fruit juice – serve with a spoonful or two of fat-free yogurt.

● One or two crisp rice cakes – delicious on their own, or topped with honey, or reduced fat cheese.

● Crackers, such as water biscuits or crisp breads, spread with reduced sugar jam or marmalade.

● A bowl of wholewheat breakfast cereal or no-added-sugar muesli served with a little skimmed milk.

● Very low fat plain or fruit yogurt or fromage frais.

● A toasted teacake spread with reduced sugar jam or marmalade.

● Toasted crumpet spread with yeast extract or beef extract.

THE FAT AND CALORIE CONTENTS OF FOOD

The following figures show the weight of fat (g) and the energy content per 100g/4oz of each food.

VEGETABLES

	FAT (g)	ENERGY		FAT (g)	ENERGY
Broccoli	0.9	33 Kcals/138 kJ	Onions	0.2	36 Kcals/151 kJ
Cabbage	0.4	26 Kcals/109 kJ	Peas	1.5	83 Kcals/344 kJ
Carrots	0.3	35 Kcals/146 kJ	Potatoes	0.2	75 Kcals/318 kJ
Cauliflower	0.9	34 Kcals/142 kJ	Chips, home-made	6.7	189 Kcals/796 kJ
Courgettes	0.4	18 Kcals/74 kJ	Chips, retail	12.4	239 Kcals/1001 kJ
Cucumber	0.1	10 Kcals/40 kJ	Oven-chips, frozen, baked	4.2	162 Kcals/687 kJ
Mushrooms	0.5	13 Kcals/55 kJ	Tomatoes	0.3	17 Kcals/73 kJ

BEANS AND PULSES

	FAT (g)	ENERGY		FAT (g)	ENERGY
Black-eyed beans, cooked	1.8	116 Kcals/494 kJ	Hummus	12.6	187 Kcals/781 kJ
Butter beans, canned	0.5	77 Kcals/327 kJ	Red kidney beans, canned	0.6	100 Kcals/424 kJ
Chick-peas, canned	2.9	115 Kcals/487 kJ	Red lentils, cooked	0.4	100 Kcals/424 kJ

FISH AND SEAFOOD

	FAT (g)	ENERGY		FAT (g)	ENERGY
Cod fillets, raw	0.7	80 Kcals/337 kJ	Prawns	0.9	99 Kcals/418 kJ
Crab, canned	0.5	77 Kcals/326 kJ	Trout, grilled	5.4	135 Kcals/565 kJ
Haddock, raw	0.6	81 Kcals/345 kJ	Tuna, canned in brine	0.6	99 Kcals/422 kJ
Lemon sole, raw	1.5	83 Kcals/351 kJ	Tuna, canned in oil	9.0	189 Kcals/794 kJ

MEAT PRODUCTS

	FAT (g)	ENERGY		FAT (g)	ENERGY
Bacon rasher, streaky	39.5	414 Kcals/1710 kJ	Chicken fillet, raw	1.1	106 Kcals/449 kJ
Turkey rasher	1.0	99 Kcals/414 kJ	Chicken, roasted	12.5	218 Kcals/910 kJ
Beef mince, raw	16.2	225 Kcals/934 kJ	Duck, meat only, raw	6.5	137 Kcals/575 kJ
Beef mince, extra lean, raw	9.6	174 Kcals/728 kJ	Duck, roasted, meat,		
Rump steak, lean and fat	10.1	174 Kcals/726 kJ	fat and skin	38.1	423 Kcals/1750 kJ
Rump steak, lean only	4.1	125 Kcals/526 kJ	Turkey, meat only, raw	1.6	105 Kcals/443 kJ
Lamb chops, loin, lean and fat	23.0	277 Kcals/1150 kJ	Liver, lamb, raw	6.2	137 Kcals/575 kJ
Lamb, average, lean, raw	8.3	156 Kcals/651 kJ	Pork pie	27.0	376 Kcals/1564 kJ
Pork chops, loin, lean and fat	21.7	270 Kcals/1119 kJ	Salami	45.2	491 Kcals/2031 kJ
Pork, average, lean, raw	4.0	123 Kcals/519 kJ	Sausage roll, flaky pastry	36.4	477 Kcals/1985 kJ

Information from *The Composition of Foods* (5th Edition 1991) is reproduced with the permission of the Royal Society of Chemistry and the Controller of Her Majesty's Stationery Office.

DAIRY, FATS AND OILS

	FAT (g)	ENERGY		FAT (g)	ENERGY
Cream, double	48.0	449 Kcals/1849 kJ	Low fat yogurt, plain	0.8	56 Kcals/236 kJ
Cream, single	19.1	198 Kcals/817 kJ	Greek yogurt	9.1	115 Kcals/477 kJ
Cream, whipping	39.3	373 Kcals/1539 kJ	Reduced fat Greek yogurt	5.0	80 Kcals/335 kJ
Crème fraîche	40.0	379 Kcals/156 kJ	Butter	81.7	737 Kcals/3031 kJ
Reduced fat crème fraîche	15.0	165 Kcals/683 kJ	Margarine	81.6	739 Kcals/3039 kJ
Reduced fat double cream	24.0	243 Kcals/1002 kJ	Low fat spread	40.5	390 Kcals/1605 kJ
Milk, skimmed	0.1	33 Kcals/130 kJ	Very low fat spread	25	273 Kcals/1128 kJ
Milk, whole	3.9	66 Kcals/275 kJ	Lard	99.0	891 Kcals/3663 kJ
Brie	26.9	319 Kcals/1323 kJ	Corn oil	99.9	899 Kcals/3696 kJ
Cheddar cheese	34.4	412 Kcals/1708 kJ	Olive oil	99.9	899 Kcals/3696 kJ
Cheddar-type, reduced fat	15.0	261 Kcals/1091 kJ	Safflower oil	99.9	899 Kcals/3696 kJ
Cream cheese	47.4	439 Kcals/1807 kJ	Eggs	10.8	147 Kcals/612 kJ
Fromage frais, plain	7.1	113 Kcals/469 kJ	Egg yolk	30.5	339 Kcals/1402 kJ
Fromage frais, very low fat	0.2	58 Kcals/247 kJ	Egg white	Trace	36 Kcals/153 kJ
Skimmed milk soft cheese	Trace	74 Kcals/313 kJ	Fat-free dressing	1.2	67 Kcals/282 kJ
Edam cheese	25.4	333 Kcals/1382 kJ	French dressing	49.4	462 Kcals/1902 kJ
Feta cheese	20.2	250 Kcals/1037 kJ	Mayonnaise	75.6	691 Kcals2843 kJ
Parmesan cheese	32.7	452 Kcals/1880 kJ	Mayonnaise, reduced calorie	28.1	288 Kcals/1188 kJ

CEREALS, BAKING AND PRESERVES

	FAT (g)	ENERGY		FAT (g)	ENERGY
Brown rice, uncooked	2.8	357 Kcals/1518 kJ	Digestive biscuit (plain)	20.9	471 Kcals/1978 kJ
White rice, uncooked	3.6	383 Kcals/1630 kJ	Reduced fat digestive biscuits	16.4	467 Kcals/1965 kJ
Pasta, white, uncooked	1.8	342 Kcals/1456 kJ	Shortbread	26.1	498 Kcals/2087 kJ
Pasta, wholemeal, uncooked	2.5	324 Kcal/1379 kJ	Madeira cake	16.9	393 Kcals/1652 kJ
Brown bread	2.0	218 Kcals/927 kJ	Fatless sponge cake	6.1	294 Kcals/1245 kJ
White bread	1.9	235 Kcals/1002 kJ	Doughnut, jam	14.5	336 Kcals/1414 kJ
Wholemeal bread	2.5	215 Kcals914 kJ	Sugar, white	0 3	94 Kcals/1680 kJ
Cornflakes	0.7	360 Kcals/1535 kJ	Chocolate, milk	30.7	520 Kcals/2177 kJ
Sultana bran	1.6	303 Kcals/1289 kJ	Chocolate, plain	28	510 Kcals/2157 kJ
Swiss-style muesli	5.9	363 Kcals/1540 kJ	Honey	0	288 Kcals/1229 kJ
Croissant	20.3	360 Kcals/1505 kJ	Lemon curd	5.0	283 Kcals/1198 kJ
Flapjack	26.6	484 Kcals/2028 kJ	Fruit jam	0 26	268 Kcals/1114 kJ

FRUIT AND NUTS

	FAT (g)	ENERGY		FAT (g)	ENERGY
Apples, eating	0.1	47 Kcals/199 kJ	Pears	0.1	40 Kcals/169 kJ
Avocados	19.5	190 Kcals/784 kJ	Almonds	55.8	612 Kcals/2534 kJ
Bananas	0.3	95 Kcals/403 kJ	Brazil nuts	68.2	682 Kcals/2813 kJ
Dried mixed fruit	0.4	268 Kcals/1114 kJ	Hazelnuts	63.5	650 Kcals/2685 kJ
Grapefruit	0.1	30 Kcals/126 kJ	Pine nuts	68.6	688 Kcals/2840 kJ
Oranges	0.1	37 Kcals/158 kJ	Walnuts	68.5	688 Kcals/2837kJ
Peaches	0.1	33 Kcals/142 kJ	Peanut butter, smooth	53.7	623 Kcals/2581 kJ

Soups
and Starters

ITALIAN VEGETABLE SOUP

The success of this clear soup depends on the quality of the stock, so for the best results, be sure you use home-made vegetable stock rather than stock cubes.

INGREDIENTS

Serves 4
1 small carrot
1 baby leek
1 celery stick
50g/2oz green cabbage
900ml/1½ pints/3¾ cups vegetable stock
1 bay leaf
115g/4oz/1 cup cooked cannellini or haricot beans
25g/1oz/⅕ cup soup pasta, such as tiny shells, bows, stars or elbows
salt and black pepper
snipped fresh chives, to garnish

1 Cut the carrot, leek and celery into 5cm/2in long julienne strips. Slice the cabbage very finely.

NUTRITION NOTES

Per portion:

Energy	69Kcals/288kJ
Protein	3.67g
Fat	0.71g
Saturated Fat	0.05g
Fibre	2.82g

2 Put the stock and bay leaf into a large saucepan and bring to the boil. Add the carrot, leek and celery, cover and simmer for 6 minutes.

3 Add the cabbage, beans and pasta shapes. Stir, then simmer uncovered for a further 4–5 minutes, or until the vegetables and pasta are tender.

4 Remove the bay leaf and season with salt and pepper to taste. Ladle into four soup bowls and garnish with snipped chives. Serve immediately.

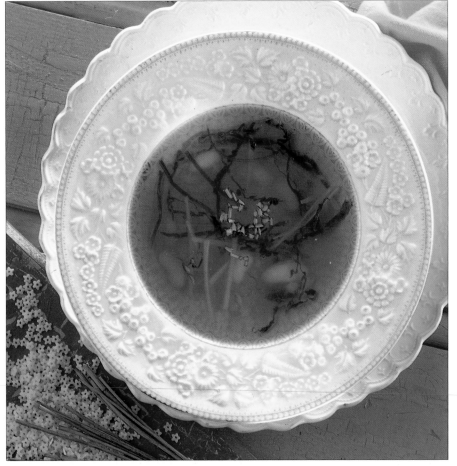

CHICKEN AND PASTA SOUP

INGREDIENTS

Serves 4–6

900ml/1½ pints/3¾ cups chicken stock
1 bay leaf
4 spring onions, sliced
225g/8oz button mushrooms, sliced
115g/4oz cooked chicken breast
50g/2oz soup pasta
150ml/¼ pint/⅔ cup dry white wine
15ml/1 tbsp chopped fresh parsley
salt and black pepper

NUTRITION NOTES

Per portion:

Energy	126Kcals/529kJ
Fat	2.2g
Saturated Fat	0.6g
Cholesterol	19mg
Fibre	1.3g

1 Put the stock and bay leaf into a pan and bring to the boil.

2 Add the spring onions and mush-rooms to the stock.

3 Remove the skin from the chicken and slice the meat thinly using a sharp knife. Add to the soup and season to taste. Heat through for about 2–3 minutes.

4 Add the pasta, cover and simmer for 7–8 minutes. Just before serving, add the wine and chopped parsley, heat through for 2–3 minutes, then season to taste.

BEETROOT SOUP WITH RAVIOLI

INGREDIENTS

Serves 4–6

1 quantity basic pasta dough (see
   page 38)
egg white, beaten, for brushing
flour, for dusting
1 small onion or shallot, finely chopped
2 garlic cloves, crushed
5ml/1 tsp fennel seeds
600ml/1 pint/2½ cups chicken stock
225g/8oz cooked beetroot
30ml/2 tbsp fresh orange juice
fennel or dill leaves, to garnish
crusty bread, to serve

For the filling

115g/4oz mushrooms, finely chopped
1 shallot or small onion, finely chopped
1–2 garlic cloves, crushed
5ml/1 tsp chopped fresh thyme
15ml/1 tbsp chopped fresh parsley
90ml/6 tbsp fresh white breadcrumbs
salt and black pepper
large pinch of ground nutmeg

1 Process all the filling ingredients and
scoop into a bowl.

NUTRITION NOTES

Per portion:

Energy	358Kcals/1504kJ
Fat	4.9g
Saturated Fat	1.0g
Cholesterol	110mg
Fibre	4.3g

2 Roll the pasta dough into thin
sheets. Lay one piece over a ravioli
tray and put a teaspoonful of the filling
into each depression. Brush around the
edges of each ravioli with egg white.
Cover with another sheet of pasta,
press the edges well together to seal
and separate the individual shapes.
Transfer to a floured dish towel and
rest for 1 hour before cooking.

3 Cook the ravioli in a large pan of
boiling, salted water for 2 minutes,
in batches to stop them sticking together. Remove and drop into a bowl of
cold water for 5 seconds before placing
on a tray. (You can make these pasta
shapes a day in advance. Cover with
clear film and store in the fridge.)

4 Put the onion, garlic and fennel
seeds into a pan with 150ml/
¼ pint/⅔ cup of the stock. Bring to the
boil, cover and simmer for 5 minutes
until tender. Peel and finely dice the
beetroot (reserve 60ml/4 tbsp for the
garnish). Add the rest of the beetroot to
the soup with the remaining stock and
bring to the boil.

5 Add the orange juice and cooked
ravioli and simmer for 2 minutes.
Pour into shallow soup bowls and
garnish with the reserved diced
beetroot and fennel or dill leaves.

SPICY TOMATO AND LENTIL SOUP

Serves 4

15ml/1 tbsp sunflower oil
1 onion, finely chopped
1–2 garlic cloves, crushed
2.5cm/1in piece fresh root ginger,
  peeled and finely chopped
5ml/1 tsp cumin seeds, crushed
450g/1lb ripe tomatoes, peeled, seeded
  and chopped
115g/4oz/½ cup red split lentils
1.2 litres/2 pints/5 cups vegetable or
  chicken stock
15ml/1 tbsp tomato purée
salt and black pepper
low fat natural yogurt and chopped
  fresh parsley, to garnish (optional)

1 Heat the sunflower oil in a large heavy-based saucepan and cook the chopped onion gently for 5 minutes until softened.

2 Stir in the garlic, ginger and cumin, followed by the tomatoes and lentils. Cook over a low heat for a further 3–4 minutes.

3 Stir in the stock and tomato purée. Bring to the boil, then lower the heat and simmer gently for about 30 minutes until the lentils are soft. Season to taste with salt and pepper.

4 Purée the soup in a blender or food processor. Return to the clean pan and reheat gently. Serve in heated bowls. If liked, garnish each portion with a swirl of yogurt and a little chopped parsley.

NUTRITION NOTES	
Per portion:	
Energy	165Kcals/695kJ
Fat	4g
Saturated Fat	0.5g
Cholesterol	0

CREAMY COD CHOWDER

A delicious light version of a classic, this chowder is a tasty combination of smoked fish, vegetables, fresh herbs and milk. To cut the calories and stock even more, use vegetable or fish stock in place of the milk. Serve as a substantial starter or snack, or as a light main meal accompanied by warm crusty wholemeal bread.

INGREDIENTS

Serves 4–6
350g/12oz smoked cod fillet
1 small onion, finely chopped
1 bay leaf
4 black peppercorns
900ml/1½ pints/3¾ cups skimmed milk
10ml/2 tsp cornflour
200g/7oz canned sweetcorn kernels
15ml/1 tbsp chopped fresh parsley

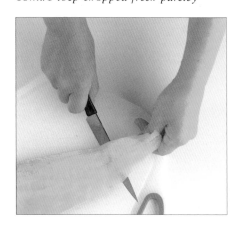

1 Skin the fish and put it into a large saucepan with the onion, bay leaf and peppercorns. Pour over the milk.

2 Bring to the boil, then reduce the heat and simmer very gently for 12–15 minutes, or until the fish is just cooked. Do not overcook.

3 Using a slotted spoon, lift out the fish and flake into large chunks. Remove the bay leaf and peppercorns and discard.

4 Blend the cornflour with 10ml/2 tsp cold water and add to the saucepan. Bring to the boil and simmer for about 1 minute or until slightly thickened.

5 Drain the sweetcorn kernels and add to the saucepan together with the flaked fish and parsley. Reheat gently and serve.

COOK'S TIP
The flavour of the chowder improves if it is made a day in advance. Leave to cool, then chill in the fridge until required. Reheat gently. Do not allow the soup to boil, or the fish will disintegrate.

NUTRITION NOTES

Per portion:
Energy	200Kcals/840kJ
Protein	24.71g
Fat	1.23g
Saturated Fat	0.32g

MELON AND BASIL SOUP

A deliciously refreshing, chilled fruit soup, just right for a hot summer's day. It takes next to no time to prepare, leaving you free to enjoy the sunshine and, even better, it is almost totally fat-free.

INGREDIENTS

Serves 4–6
2 Charentais or rock melons
75g/3oz/6 tbsp caster sugar
175ml/6fl oz/³/₄ cup water
finely grated rind and juice of 1 lime
45ml/3 tbsp shredded fresh basil
fresh basil leaves, to garnish

1 Cut the melons in half across the middle. Scrape out the seeds and discard. Using a melon baller, scoop out 20–24 balls and set aside for the garnish. Scoop out the remaining flesh and place in a blender or food processor. Set aside.

2 Place the sugar, water and lime zest in a small pan over a low heat. Stir until dissolved, bring to the boil and simmer for 2–3 minutes. Remove from the heat and leave to cool slightly. Pour half the mixture into the blender or food processor with the melon flesh. Blend until smooth, adding the remaining syrup and lime juice to taste.

3 Pour the mixture into a bowl, stir in the basil and chill. Serve garnished with basil leaves and melon balls.

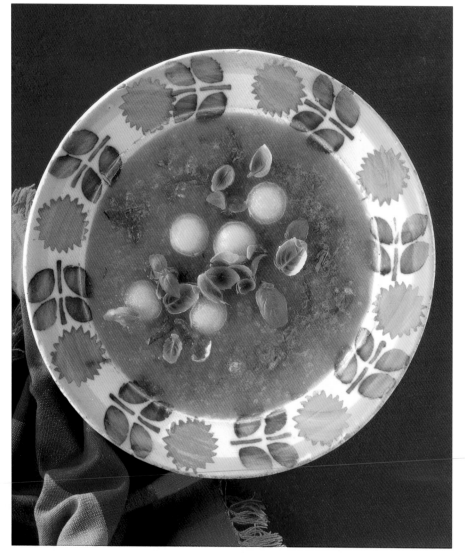

NUTRITION NOTES	
Per portion:	
Energy	69Kcals/293.8kJ
Fat	0.14g
Saturated Fat	0
Cholesterol	0
Fibre	0.47g

COOK'S TIP
Add the syrup in two stages, as the amount of sugar needed will depend on the sweetness of the melon.

CHILLED FRESH TOMATO SOUP

This effortless uncooked soup can be made in minutes.

INGREDIENTS

Serves 6
1.5kg/3–3½lb ripe tomatoes, peeled and
roughly chopped
4 garlic cloves, crushed
30ml/2 tbsp balsamic vinegar
4 thick slices wholemeal bread
black pepper
low fat fromage frais, to garnish

1 Place the tomatoes in a blender with the garlic. Blend until smooth.

2 Pass the mixture through a sieve to remove the seeds. Stir in balsamic vinegar and season to taste with pepper. Put in the fridge to chill.

3 Toast the bread lightly on both sides. While still hot, cut off the crusts and slice the toast in half horizontally. Place on a board with the uncooked sides facing down and, using a circular motion, rub to remove any doughy pieces of bread.

COOK'S TIP
For the best flavour, it is important to use only fully ripened, flavourful tomatoes in this soup.

4 Cut each slice into four triangles. Place on a grill pan and toast the uncooked sides until lightly golden. Garnish each bowl of soup with a spoonful of fromage frais and serve with the Melba toast.

NUTRITION NOTES

Per portion:
Energy	111Kcals/475kJ
Fat	1.42g
Saturated Fat	0.39g
Cholesterol	0.16mg
Fibre	4.16g

MINTED MELON AND GRAPEFRUIT

Melon is always a popular starter. Here the succulent flavour of the Galia melon is complemented by the refreshing taste of citrus fruit and a simple mustard and vinegar dressing. Fresh mint, used in the cocktail and as a garnish, enhances both its flavour and appearance.

INGREDIENTS

Serves 4
1 small Galia melon, weighing about
    1kg/2¼lb
2 pink grapefruit
1 yellow grapefruit
5ml/1 tsp Dijon mustard
5ml/1 tsp raspberry or sherry vinegar
5ml/1 tsp clear honey
15ml/1 tbsp chopped fresh mint
sprigs of fresh mint,
    to garnish

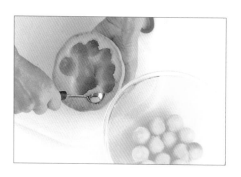

1 Halve the melon and remove the seeds with a teaspoon. With a melon baller, carefully scoop the flesh into balls.

NUTRITION NOTES

Per portion:

Energy	97Kcals/409kJ
Protein	2.22g
Fat	0.63g
Saturated Fat	0
Fibre	3.05g

2 With a small sharp knife, peel the grapefruit and remove all the white pith. Remove the segments by cutting between the membranes, holding the fruit over a small bowl to catch any juices.

3 Whisk the mustard, vinegar, honey, chopped mint and grapefruit juices together in a mixing bowl. Add the melon balls together with the grapefruit and mix well. Chill for 30 minutes.

4 Ladle the fruit into four glass dishes and serve garnished with sprigs of fresh mint.

GUACAMOLE WITH CRUDITÉS

This fresh-tasting spicy dip is made using peas instead of the avocado pears that are traditionally associated with this dish. This version saves on both fat and calories, without compromising on taste.

INGREDIENTS

Serves 4–6
350g/12oz/2¼ cups frozen peas, defrosted
1 garlic clove, crushed
2 spring onions, chopped
5ml/1 tsp finely grated rind and juice of 1 lime
2.5ml/½ tsp ground cumin
dash of Tabasco sauce
15ml/1 tbsp reduced fat mayonnaise
30ml/2 tbsp chopped fresh coriander or parsley
salt and black pepper
pinch of paprika and lime slices, to garnish

For the crudités
6 baby carrots
2 celery sticks
1 red-skinned eating apple
1 pear
15ml/1 tbsp lemon or lime juice
6 baby sweetcorn

2 Add the chopped coriander or parsley and process for a few more seconds. Spoon into a serving bowl, cover with clear film and chill in the fridge for 30 minutes, to let the flavours develop fully.

3 For the crudités, trim and peel the carrots. Halve the celery sticks lengthways and trim into sticks, the same length as the carrots. Quarter, core and thickly slice the apple and pear, then dip into the lemon or lime juice. Arrange with the baby sweetcorn on a platter.

NUTRITION NOTES

Per portion:
Energy	110Kcals/460kJ
Protein	6.22g
Fat	2.29g
Saturated Fat	0.49g
Fibre	6.73g

COOK'S TIP
Serve the guacamole dip with warmed wholemeal pitta bread.

1 Put the peas, garlic clove, spring onions, lime rind and juice, cumin, Tabasco sauce, mayonnaise and salt and black pepper into a food processor or a blender for a few minutes and process until smooth.

4 Sprinkle the paprika over the guacamole and garnish with twisted lime slices.

TZATZIKI

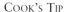

Tzatziki is a Greek cucumber salad dressed with yogurt, mint and garlic. It is typically served with grilled lamb and chicken, but is also good served with crudités.

INGREDIENTS

Serves 4
1 cucumber
5ml/1 tsp salt
45ml/3 tbsp finely chopped fresh mint, plus a few sprigs to garnish
1 garlic clove, crushed
5ml/1 tsp caster sugar
200ml/7fl oz reduced fat Greek-style yogurt
cucumber flower, to garnish (optional)

1 Peel the cucumber. Reserve a little of the cucumber to use as a garnish if you wish and cut the rest in half lengthways. Remove the seeds with a teaspoon and discard. Slice the cucumber thinly and combine with salt. Leave for approximately 15–20 minutes. Salt will soften the cucumber and draw out any bitter juices.

COOK'S TIP
If you want to prepare Tzatziki in a hurry, then leave out the method for salting cucumber at the end of step 1. The cucumber will have a more crunchy texture, and will be slightly less sweet.

2 Combine the mint, garlic, sugar and yogurt in a bowl, reserving a few sprigs of mint as decoration.

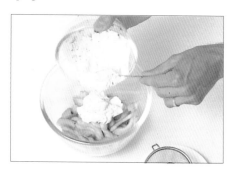

3 Rinse the cucumber in a sieve under cold running water to flush away the salt. Drain well and combine with the yogurt. Decorate with cucumber flower and/or mint. Serve cold.

NUTRITION NOTES
Per portion:
Energy	41.5Kcals/174.5kJ
Fat	0.51g
Saturated Fat	0.25g
Cholesterol	2mg
Fibre	0.2g

CHILLI TOMATO SALSA

This universal dip is great served with absolutely anything and can be made up to 24 hours in advance.

INGREDIENTS

Serves 4
1 shallot, peeled and halved
2 garlic cloves, peeled
handful of fresh basil leaves
500g/1¼ lb ripe tomatoes
10ml/2 tsp olive oil
2 green chillies
salt and black pepper

1 Place the shallot and garlic in a food processor with the fresh basil. Whizz the shallot, garlic and basil until finely chopped.

2 Halve the tomatoes and add to the food processor. Pulse the machine until the mixture is well blended and coarsely chopped.

3 With the motor running, slowly pour in the olive oil. Add salt and pepper to taste.

NUTRITION NOTES	
Per portion:	
Energy	28Kcals/79kJ
Fat	0.47g
Saturated Fat	0.13g
Cholesterol	0
Fibre	1.45g

4 Halve the chillies lengthways and remove the seeds. Finely slice the chillies widthways into tiny strips and stir into the tomato salsa. Serve at room temperature.

COOK'S TIP
The salsa is best made in the summer when tomatoes are at their best. In winter, use a drained 400g/14oz can of plum tomatoes.

FRESH FIG, APPLE AND DATE SALAD

Sweet Mediterranean figs and dates combine especially well with crisp eating apples. A hint of almond serves to unite the flavours, but if you'd prefer to reduce the fat even more, omit the marzipan and add another 30ml/2 tbsp low fat natural yogurt or use low fat fromage frais instead.

INGREDIENTS

Serves 4
6 large eating apples
juice of ½ lemon
175g/6oz fresh dates
25g/1oz white marzipan
5ml/1 tsp orange flower water
60ml/4 tbsp low fat natural yogurt
4 green or purple figs
4 almonds, toasted

1 Core the apples. Slice thinly, then cut into fine matchsticks. Moisten with lemon juice to keep them white.

NUTRITION NOTES

Per portion:
Energy	255Kcals/876.5kJ
Fat	4.98g
Saturated Fat	1.05g
Cholesterol	2.25mg
Fibre	1.69g

2 Remove the stones from the dates and cut the flesh into fine strips, then combine with the apple slices.

3 Soften the marzipan with orange flower water and combine with the yogurt. Mix well.

COOK'S TIP
For a slightly stronger almond flavour, add a few drops of almond essence to the yogurt mixture. When buying fresh figs, choose firm, unblemished fruit which give slightly when lightly squeezed. Avoid damaged, bruised or very soft fruit.

4 Pile the apples and dates in the centre of four plates. Remove the stem from each of the figs and divide the fruit into quarters without cutting right through the base. Squeeze the base with the thumb and forefinger of each hand to open up the fruit.

5 Place a fig in the centre of each salad. Spoon the yogurt filling on to the figs and decorate each one with a toasted almond.

Vegetarian
Dishes

TAGLIATELLE WITH MUSHROOMS

INGREDIENTS

Serves 4

1 small onion, finely chopped
2 garlic cloves, crushed
150ml/¼ pint/⅔ cup vegetable stock
225g/8oz mixed fresh mushrooms, such
    as field, chestnut, oyster or
    chanterelles
60ml/4 tbsp white or red wine
10ml/2 tsp tomato purée
15ml/1 tbsp soy sauce
5ml/1 tsp chopped fresh thyme
30ml/2 tbsp chopped fresh parsley, plus
    extra to garnish
225g/8oz fresh sun-dried tomato and
    herb tagliatelle
salt and black pepper
shavings of Parmesan cheese, to serve
    (optional)

1 Put the onion and garlic into a pan with the stock, then cover and cook for 5 minutes or until tender.

NUTRITION NOTES	
Per portion:	
Energy	241Kcals/1010kJ
Fat	2.4g
Saturated Fat	0.7g
Carbohydrate	45g
Fibre	3g

2 Add the mushrooms (quartered or sliced if large or left whole if small), wine, tomato purée and soy sauce. Cover and cook for 5 minutes.

3 Remove the lid from the pan and boil until the liquid has reduced by half. Stir in the chopped fresh herbs and season to taste.

4 Cook the fresh pasta in a large pan of boiling, salted water for 2–5 minutes until *al dente*. Drain thoroughly and toss lightly with the mushrooms. Serve, garnished with parsley and shavings of Parmesan cheese, if you like.

PASTA PRIMAVERA

You can use any mixture of fresh, young spring vegetables to make this delicately flavoured pasta dish.

INGREDIENTS

Serves 4

225g/8oz thin asparagus spears, chopped in half
115g/4oz mange-tout, topped and tailed
115g/4oz baby sweetcorn
225g/8oz whole baby carrots, trimmed
1 small red pepper, seeded and chopped
8 spring onions, sliced
225g/8oz torchietti or other pasta shapes
150ml/¼ pint/⅔ cup low fat cottage cheese
150ml/¼ pint/⅔ cup low fat yogurt
15ml/1 tbsp lemon juice
15ml/1 tbsp chopped parsley
15ml/1 tbsp snipped chives
skimmed milk (optional)
salt and black pepper
sun-dried tomato bread, to serve

1 Cook the asparagus spears in a pan of boiling, salted water for 3–4 minutes. Add the mange-tout halfway through the cooking time. Drain and rinse both under cold water to stop further cooking.

2 Cook the baby corn, carrots, red pepper and spring onions in the same way until tender. Drain and rinse.

3 Cook the pasta in a large pan of boiling, salted water according to the packet instruction, until *al dente*. Drain thoroughly.

4 Put the cottage cheese, yogurt, lemon juice, parsley, chives and seasoning into a food processor or blender and process until smooth. Thin the sauce with skimmed milk, if necessary. Put into a large pan with the pasta and vegetables, heat gently and toss carefully. Serve at once with sun-dried tomato bread.

NUTRITION NOTES

Per portion:

Energy	320Kcals/1344kJ
Fat	3.1g
Saturated Fat	0.4g
Cholesterol	3mg
Fibre	6.2g

SPAGHETTI WITH CHILLI BEAN SAUCE

A nutritious vegetarian option, ideal as a low fat main course.

INGREDIENTS

Serves 6

1 onion, finely chopped
1–2 garlic cloves, crushed
1 large green chilli, seeded
  and chopped
150ml/¼ pint/⅔ cup vegetable stock
400g/14oz can chopped tomatoes
30ml/2 tbsp tomato purée
120ml/4fl oz/½ cup red wine
5ml/1 tsp dried oregano
200g/7oz French beans, sliced
400g/14oz can red kidney
  beans, drained
400g/14oz can cannellini
  beans, drained
400g/14oz can chick-peas, drained
450g/1lb spaghetti
salt and black pepper

1 To make the sauce, put the chopped onion, garlic and chilli into a non-stick pan with the stock. Bring to the boil and cook for 5 minutes until tender.

2 Add the tomatoes, tomato purée, wine, seasoning and oregano. Bring to the boil, cover and simmer the sauce for 20 minutes.

3 Cook the French beans in boiling, salted water for about 5–6 minutes until tender. Drain thoroughly.

4 Add all the beans and the chick-peas to the sauce and simmer for a further 10 minutes. Meanwhile, cook the spaghetti in a large pan of boiling, salted water according to the individual packet instructions, until *al dente*. Drain thoroughly. Transfer the pasta to a serving dish or plates and top with the chilli bean sauce.

> COOK'S TIP
> Rinse canned beans thoroughly under cold, running water to remove as much salt as possible and drain well before use.

LENTIL BOLOGNESE

A really useful sauce to serve with pasta, as a pancake stuffing or even as a protein-packed sauce for vegetables.

INGREDIENTS

Serves 6
45ml/3 tbsp olive oil
1 onion, chopped
2 garlic cloves, crushed
2 carrots, coarsely grated
2 celery sticks, chopped
115g/4oz/²/₃ cup red lentils
400g/14oz can chopped tomatoes
30ml/2 tbsp tomato purée
450ml/³/₄ pint/2 cups stock
15ml/1 tbsp fresh marjoram, chopped, or 5ml/1 tsp dried marjoram
salt and black pepper

1 Heat the oil in a large saucepan and gently fry the onion, garlic, carrots and celery for about 5 minutes, until they are soft.

NUTRITION NOTES

Per portion:	
Energy	103Kcals/432kJ
Fat	2.19g
Saturated Fat	0.85g
Fibre	2.15g

2 Add the lentils, tomatoes, tomato purée, stock, marjoram and seasoning to the pan.

3 Bring the mixture to the boil, then partially cover with a lid and simmer for 20 minutes until thick and soft. Use the sauce as required.

COOK'S TIP
You can easily reduce the fat in this recipe by using less olive oil, or substituting a little of the stock and cooking the vegetables over a low heat in a non-stick frying pan until they are soft.

SWEET AND SOUR PEPPERS WITH PASTA

A tasty and colourful low fat dish – perfect for lunch or supper.

INGREDIENTS

Serves 4
1 red, 1 yellow and 1 orange pepper
1 garlic clove, crushed
30ml/2 tbsp capers
30ml/2 tbsp raisins
5ml/1 tsp wholegrain mustard
rind and juice of 1 lime
5ml/1 tsp clear honey
30ml/2 tbsp chopped fresh coriander
225g/8oz pasta bows
salt and black pepper
shavings of Parmesan cheese, to serve
    (optional)

1 Quarter the peppers and remove the stalks and seeds. Put the quarters into boiling water and cook for 10–15 minutes, until tender. Drain and rinse under cold water, then peel off the skin and cut the flesh into strips lengthways.

2 Put the garlic, capers, raisins, mustard, lime rind and juice, honey, coriander and seasoning into a bowl and whisk together.

3 Cook the pasta in a large pan of boiling, salted water for 10–12 minutes, until *al dente*. Drain thoroughly.

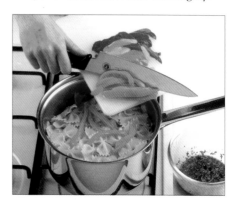

4 Return the pasta to the pan and add the pepper strips and dressing. Heat gently, tossing to mix. Transfer to a warm serving bowl and serve with a few shavings of Parmesan cheese, if using.

NUTRITION NOTES	
Per portion:	
Energy	268Kcals/1125kJ
Fat	2.0g
Saturated Fat	0.5g
Cholesterol	1.3mg
Fibre	4.3g

PASTA WITH CHICK-PEA SAUCE

This is a delicious, and very speedy, low fat dish. The quality of canned pulses and tomatoes is so good that it is possible to transform them into a very fresh tasting pasta sauce in minutes. Choose whatever pasta shapes you like, although hollow shapes, such as penne (quills) or shells are particularly good with this sauce.

INGREDIENTS

Serves 6

450g/1lb penne or other pasta shapes
30ml/2 tsp olive oil
1 onion, thinly sliced
1 red pepper, seeded and sliced
400g/14oz can chopped tomatoes
425g/15oz can chick-peas
30ml/2 tbsp dry vermouth (optional)
5ml/1 tsp dried oregano
1 large bay leaf
30ml/2 tbsp capers
salt and black pepper
fresh oregano, to garnish

COOK'S TIP
Choose fresh or dried unfilled pasta for this dish. Whichever you choose, cook it in a large saucepan of water, so that the pasta keeps separate and doesn't stick together. Fresh pasta takes about 2–4 minutes to cook and dried pasta about 8–10 minutes. Cook pasta until it is *al dente* – firm and neither too hard nor too soft.

NUTRITION NOTES

Per portion:	
Energy	268Kcals/1125kJ
Fat	2.0g
Saturated Fat	0.5g
Cholesterol	1.3mg
Fibre	4.3g

1 Boil the pasta as instructed on the packet, then drain. Meanwhile, heat the oil in a large saucepan and gently fry the onion and pepper for about 5 minutes, stirring occasionally, until softened.

2 Add the tomatoes, chick-peas with their liquid, vermouth (if liked), herbs and capers and stir well.

3 Season to taste and bring to the boil, then simmer for about 10 minutes. Remove the bay leaf and mix in the pasta. Reheat and serve hot, garnished with sprigs of oregano.

PAPPARDELLE AND PROVENÇAL SAUCE

INGREDIENTS

Serves 4

2 small red onions
150ml/¼ pint/⅔ cup vegetable stock
1–2 garlic cloves, crushed
60ml/4 tbsp red wine
2 courgettes, cut in fingers
1 yellow pepper, seeded and sliced
400g/14oz can tomatoes
10ml/2 tsp fresh thyme
5ml/1 tsp caster sugar
350g/12oz pappardelle or other
   ribbon pasta
salt and black pepper
fresh thyme and 6 black olives, stoned
   and roughly chopped, to garnish

NUTRITION NOTES

Per portion:

Energy	369Kcals/1550kJ
Fat	2.5g
Saturated Fat	0.4g
Cholesterol	0
Fibre	4.3g

1 Cut each onion into eight wedges through the root end, to hold them together during cooking. Put into a saucepan with the stock and garlic. Bring to the boil, cover and simmer for 5 minutes until tender.

2 Add the red wine, courgettes, yellow pepper, tomatoes, thyme, sugar and seasoning. Bring to the boil and cook gently for 5–7 minutes, shaking the pan occasionally to coat the vegetables with the sauce. (Do not overcook the vegetables as they are much nicer if they remain slightly crunchy.)

3 Cook the pasta in a large pan of boiling, salted water according to the packet instructions, until *al dente*. Drain thoroughly.

4 Transfer the pasta to warmed serving plates and top with the vegetables. Garnish with fresh thyme and chopped black olives.

BASIC PASTA DOUGH

To make fresh pasta, sift 200g/7oz/1¾ cups plain flour and a pinch of salt on to a work surface and make a well in the centre. Break two eggs into the well, together with 10ml/2 tsp of cold water. Using a fork, beat the eggs gently, then gradually draw in the flour from the sides to make a thick paste. When the mixture becomes too stiff to use a fork, use your hands to mix to a firm dough. Knead for 5 minutes until smooth. Wrap in clear film and leave to rest for 20–30 minutes before rolling out and cutting.

CRACKED WHEAT AND MINT SALAD

INGREDIENTS

Serves 4

250g/9oz/1²⁄₃ cups cracked wheat
4 tomatoes
4 small courgettes, thinly sliced
   lengthways
4 spring onions, sliced on the diagonal
8 ready-to-eat dried apricots, chopped
40g/1¹⁄₂oz/¹⁄₄ cup raisins
juice of 1 lemon
30ml/2 tbsp tomato juice
45ml/3 tbsp chopped fresh mint
1 garlic clove, crushed
salt and black pepper
sprig of fresh mint, to garnish

1 Put the cracked wheat into a large bowl. Add enough boiling water to come 2.5cm/1in above the level of the wheat. Leave to soak for 30 minutes, then drain well and squeeze out any excess water in a clean dish towel.

2 Meanwhile, plunge the tomatoes into boiling water for 1 minute and then into cold water. Slip off the skins. Halve, remove the seeds and cores and roughly chop the flesh.

3 Stir the chopped tomatoes, courgettes, spring onions, apricots and raisins into the cracked wheat.

NUTRITION NOTES

Per portion:

Energy	293Kcals/1231.7kJ
Fat	1.69g
Saturated Fat	0.28g
Fibre	2.25g

4 Put the lemon and tomato juice, mint, garlic clove and seasoning into a small bowl and whisk together with a fork. Pour over the salad and mix well. Chill for at least 1 hour. Serve garnished with a sprig of mint.

CHILLI BEAN BAKE

The contrasting textures of sauce, beans, vegetables and a crunchy cornbread topping make this a memorable meal.

— INGREDIENTS —

Serves 4

225g/8oz/1¼ cups red kidney beans
1 bay leaf
1 large onion, finely chopped
1 garlic clove, crushed
2 celery sticks, sliced
5ml/1 tsp ground cumin
5ml/1 tsp chilli powder
400g/14oz can chopped tomatoes
15ml/1 tbsp tomato purée
5ml/1 tsp dried mixed herbs
15ml/1 tbsp lemon juice
1 yellow pepper, seeded and diced
salt and black pepper
mixed salad, to serve

For the cornbread topping

175g/6oz/1½ cups corn meal
15ml/1 tbsp wholemeal flour
5ml/1 tsp baking powder
1 egg, beaten
175ml/6fl oz/¾ cup skimmed milk

1 Soak the beans overnight in cold water. Drain and rinse well. Pour 1 litre/1¾ pints/4 cups water into a large, heavy-based saucepan, add the beans and bay leaf and boil rapidly for 10 minutes. Lower the heat, cover and simmer for 35–40 minutes or until the beans are tender.

— NUTRITION NOTES —

Per portion:

Energy	399Kcals/1675kJ
Protein	22.86g
Fat	4.65g
Saturated Fat	0.86g
Fibre	11.59g

2 Add the onion, garlic, celery, cumin, chilli powder, chopped tomatoes, tomato purée and dried mixed herbs. Half cover the pan with a lid and simmer for a further 10 minutes.

3 Stir in the lemon juice, yellow pepper and seasoning. Simmer for a further 8–10 minutes, stirring occasionally, until the vegetables are just tender. Discard the bay leaf and spoon the mixture into a large casserole.

4 Preheat the oven to 220°C/425°F/Gas 7. To make the topping, put the corn meal, flour, baking powder and a pinch of salt into a bowl and mix together. Make a well in the centre and add the egg and milk. Mix and pour over the bean mixture. Bake in the oven for 20 minutes or until brown. Serve hot with mixed salad.

SPICY BEAN HOT POT

INGREDIENTS

Serves 4

225g/8oz/3 cups button mushrooms
15ml/1 tbsp sunflower oil
2 onions, sliced
1 garlic clove, crushed
15ml/1 tbsp red wine vinegar
400g/14oz can chopped tomatoes
15ml/1 tbsp tomato purée
15ml/1 tbsp Worcestershire sauce
15ml/1 tbsp wholegrain mustard
15ml/1 tbsp soft dark brown sugar
250ml/8fl oz/1 cup vegetable stock
400g/14oz can red kidney
    beans, drained
400g/14oz can haricot or cannellini
    beans, drained
1 bay leaf
75g/3oz/½ cup raisins
salt and black pepper
chopped fresh parsley, to garnish

1 Wipe the mushrooms, then cut them into small pieces. Set aside.

2 Heat the oil in a large saucepan or flameproof casserole, add the onions and garlic and cook over a gentle heat for 10 minutes until soft.

3 Add all the remaining ingredients except the mushrooms and seasoning. Bring to the boil, lower the heat and simmer for 10 minutes.

4 Add the mushrooms and simmer for 5 minutes more. Stir in salt and pepper to taste. Transfer to warm plates and sprinkle with parsley.

NUTRITION NOTES	
Per portion:	
Energy	280Kcals/1175kJ
Fat	4.5g
Saturated Fat	0.5g
Cholesterol	0

RATATOUILLE PANCAKES

These pancakes are made slightly thicker than usual to hold the juicy vegetable filling. By using cooking spray, you can control the amount of fat you are using and keep it to a minimum.

INGREDIENTS

Serves 4

75g/3oz/²/₃ cup plain flour
pinch of salt
25g/1oz/¹/₄ cup medium oatmeal
1 egg
300ml/¹/₂ pint/1¹/₄ cups skimmed milk
non-stick cooking spray
mixed salad, to serve

For the filling
*1 large aubergine, cut into 2.5cm/
  1in cubes*
1 garlic clove, crushed
2 medium courgettes, sliced
1 green pepper, seeded and sliced
1 red pepper, seeded and sliced
75ml/5 tbsp vegetable stock
200g/7oz can chopped tomatoes
5ml/1 tsp cornflour
salt and black pepper

NUTRITION NOTES

Per portion:

Energy	182Kcals/767kJ
Protein	9.36g
Fat	3.07g
Saturated Fat	0.62g
Fibre	4.73g

COOK'S TIP
Adding oatmeal to the batter mixture adds flavour, colour and texture to the cooked pancakes. If you like, wholemeal flour may be used in place of white flour to add extra fibre and flavour too.

1 Sift the flour and a pinch of salt into a bowl. Stir in the oatmeal. Make a well in the centre, add the egg and half the milk and mix to a smooth batter. Gradually beat in the remaining milk. Cover the bowl and leave to stand for 30 minutes.

2 Spray an 18cm/7in heavy-based frying pan with cooking spray. Heat the pan, then pour in just enough batter to cover the base of the pan thinly. Cook for 2–3 minutes, until the underside is golden brown. Flip over and cook for a further 1–2 minutes.

3 Slide the pancake out on to a plate lined with non-stick baking paper. Stack the other pancakes on top as they are made, interleaving each with non-stick baking paper. Keep warm.

4 For the filling, put the aubergine in a colander and sprinkle well with salt. Leave to stand on a plate for 30 minutes. Rinse thoroughly and drain well.

5 Put the garlic clove, courgettes, peppers, stock and tomatoes into a large saucepan. Simmer uncovered, stirring occasionally, for 10 minutes. Add the aubergine and cook for a further 15 minutes. Blend the cornflour with 10ml/2 tsp water and stir into the saucepan. Simmer for 2 minutes. Season to taste.

6 Spoon some of the ratatouille mixture into the middle of each pancake. Fold each one in half, then in half again to make a cone shape. Serve hot with a mixed salad.

Vegetarian Cassoulet

Every town in south-west France has its own version of this popular classic. Warm French bread is all that you need to accompany this hearty low fat vegetable version.

Ingredients

Serves 4–6
400g/14oz/2 cups dried haricot beans
1 bay leaf
2 onions
3 whole cloves
2 garlic cloves, crushed
5ml/1 tsp olive oil
2 leeks, thickly sliced
12 baby carrots
115g/4oz button mushrooms
400g/14oz can chopped tomatoes
15ml/1 tbsp tomato purée
5ml/1 tsp paprika
15ml/1 tbsp chopped fresh thyme
30ml/2 tbsp chopped fresh parsley
115g/4oz/2 cups fresh white
  breadcrumbs
salt and black pepper

Nutrition Notes

Per portion:
Energy	325Kcals/1378kJ
Fat	3.08g
Saturated Fat	0.46g
Cholesterol	0
Fibre	15.68g

Cook's Tip

If you're short of time, use canned haricot beans – you'll need two 400g/14oz cans. Drain, reserving the bean juices and make up to 400ml/14fl oz/1²/₃ cups with vegetable stock.

1 Soak the beans overnight in plenty of cold water. Drain and rinse under cold running water. Put them in a saucepan with 1.75 litres/3 pints/7½ cups of cold water and the bay leaf. Bring to the boil and cook rapidly for 10 minutes.

2 Peel one of the onions and spike with the cloves. Add to the beans, then reduce the heat. Cover and simmer gently for 1 hour, until the beans are almost tender. Drain, reserving the stock but discarding the bay leaf and onion.

3 Chop the remaining onion and put it into a large flameproof casserole together with the crushed garlic and olive oil. Cook gently for 5 minutes, or until softened.

4 Preheat the oven to 160°C/325°F/Gas 3. Add the leeks, carrots, mushrooms, chopped tomatoes, tomato purée, paprika and thyme to the casserole, then pour in about 400ml/14fl oz/1²/₃ cups of the reserved stock.

5 Bring to the boil, cover and simmer gently for 10 minutes. Stir in the cooked beans and parsley. Season to taste with salt and pepper.

6 Sprinkle the breadcrumbs over the top and bake uncovered for 35 minutes or until the topping is golden brown and crisp.

VEGETABLE BIRYANI

This exotic dish made from everyday ingredients will be appreciated by vegetarians and meat-eaters alike. It is extremely low in fat, but packed full of exciting flavours.

INGREDIENTS

Serves 4–6

175g/6oz/1 cup long grain rice
2 whole cloves
seeds of 2 cardamom pods
450ml/³⁄4 pint/scant 2 cups vegetable
   stock
2 garlic cloves
1 small onion, roughly chopped
5ml/1 tsp cumin seeds
5ml/1 tsp ground coriander
2.5ml/¹⁄2 tsp ground turmeric
2.5ml/¹⁄2 tsp chilli powder
1 large potato, peeled and cut into
   2.5cm/1in cubes
2 carrots, sliced
¹⁄2 cauliflower, broken into florets
50g/2oz French beans, cut into
   2.5cm/1in lengths
30ml/2 tbsp chopped fresh coriander
30ml/2 tbsp lime juice
salt and black pepper
sprig of fresh coriander, to garnish

COOK'S TIP
Substitute other vegetables, if you like. Courgettes, broccoli, parsnip and sweet potatoes would all be excellent choices.

4 Preheat the oven to 180°C/350°F/ Gas 4. Spoon the spicy paste into a flameproof casserole and cook over a low heat for 2 minutes, stirring occasionally.

5 Add the potato, carrots, cauliflower florets, beans and 90ml/6 tbsp water. Cover and cook over a low heat for a further 12 minutes, stirring occasionally. Add the chopped coriander.

2 Reduce the heat, cover and simmer for 20 minutes, or until all the stock has been absorbed.

1 Put the rice, cloves and cardamom seeds into a large, heavy-based saucepan. Pour over the stock and bring to the boil.

3 Meanwhile put the garlic cloves, onion, cumin seeds, coriander, turmeric, chilli powder and seasoning into a blender or coffee grinder together with 30ml/2 tbsp water. Blend to a smooth paste.

6 Remove the cloves and spoon the rice over the vegetables. Sprinkle over the lime juice. Cover and cook in the oven for 25 minutes, or until the vegetables are tender. Fluff up the rice with a fork before serving and garnish with a sprig of fresh coriander.

Meat
and Poultry

BARBECUED CHICKEN

INGREDIENTS

Serves 4 or 8

8 small chicken pieces
2 limes, cut into wedges, 2 red chillies,
  finely sliced, and 2 lemon grass
  stalks, to garnish
rice, to serve

For the marinade

2 lemon grass stalks, chopped
2.5cm/1in piece fresh root ginger
6 garlic cloves
4 shallots
1/2 bunch coriander roots
15ml/1 tbsp palm sugar
120ml/4fl oz/1/2 cup coconut milk
30ml/2 tbsp fish sauce
30ml/2 tbsp soy sauce

COOK'S TIP
Don't eat the skin of the chicken –
it's only left on to keep the flesh
moist during cooking. Coconut
milk makes a good base for a
marinade or sauce, as it is low in
calories and fat.

NUTRITION NOTES

Per portion (for 8):
Energy	106Kcals/449kJ
Fat	2.05g
Saturated Fat	1.10g
Cholesterol	1.10mg
Fibre	109g

1 To make the marinade, put all the
ingredients into a food processor
and process until smooth.

2 Put the chicken pieces in a dish and
pour over the marinade. Leave in a
cool place to marinate for at least
4 hours or overnight.

3 Preheat the oven to 200°C/400°F/
Gas 6. Put the chicken pieces on a
rack on a baking tray. Brush with
marinade and bake in the oven for
about 20–30 minutes or until the
chicken is cooked and golden brown.
Turn the pieces over halfway through
and brush with more marinade.

4 Garnish with lime wedges, finely
sliced red chillies and lemon grass
stalks. Serve with rice.

TANDOORI CHICKEN KEBABS

This dish originates from the plains of the Punjab at the foot of the Himalayas, where food is traditionally cooked in clay ovens known as tandoors – hence the name.

INGREDIENTS

Serves 4

4 boneless, skinless chicken breasts
(about 130g/3½oz each)
15ml/1 tbsp lemon juice
45ml/3 tbsp tandoori paste
45ml/3 tbsp low fat natural yogurt
1 garlic clove, crushed
30ml/2 tbsp chopped fresh coriander
1 small onion, cut into wedges and
separated into layers
10ml/1 tsp oil, for brushing
salt and black pepper
fresh coriander sprigs, to garnish
pilau rice and naan bread, to serve

1 Chop the chicken breasts into 2.5cm/1in cubes, put in a bowl and add the lemon juice, tandoori paste, yogurt, garlic, coriander and seasoning. Cover and leave to marinate in the fridge for 2–3 hours.

2 Preheat the grill to high. Thread alternate pieces of chicken and onion on to four skewers.

COOK'S TIP
Use chopped, boned and skinned chicken thighs, or strips of turkey breasts, for a cheaper and equally low fat alternative.

3 Brush the onions with a little oil, lay the skewers on a grill rack and cook for 10–12 minutes, turning once.

4 Garnish the kebabs with coriander and serve at once with pilau rice and naan bread.

NUTRITION NOTES

Per portion:

Energy	215.7Kcals/911.2kJ
Fat	4.2g
Saturated Fat	0.27g
Cholesterol	122mg
Fibre	0.22g

CHICKEN, CARROT AND LEEK PARCELS

These intriguing parcels may sound a bit fiddly for everyday eating, but actually they take very little time, and you can freeze them ready to cook from frozen when needed.

INGREDIENTS

Serves 4
4 *chicken fillets or skinless, boneless*
  breast portions
2 *small leeks, sliced*
2 *carrots, grated*
2 *stoned black olives, chopped*
1 *garlic clove, crushed*
4 *anchovy fillets, halved lengthways*
salt and black pepper
black olives and herb sprigs, to garnish

1 Preheat the oven to 200°C/400°F/ Gas 6. Season the chicken well.

2 Cut out four sheets of lightly greased greaseproof paper about 23cm/9in square. Divide the leeks equally among them. Put a piece of chicken on top of each.

3 Mix the carrots, olives and garlic together. Season lightly and place on top of the chicken portions. Top each with two of the anchovy fillets.

4 Carefully wrap up each parcel, making sure the paper folds are sealed. Bake the parcels for 20 minutes and serve hot, in the paper, garnished with black olives and herb sprigs.

NUTRITION NOTES

Per portion:
Energy	154Kcals/651kJ
Fat	2.37g
Saturated Fat	0.45g
Cholesterol	78.75mg
Fibre	2.1g

COOK'S TIP
Skinless, boneless chicken is low in fat and is an excellent source of protein. Small, skinless turkey breast fillets also work well in this recipe and make a tasty change.

RAGOÛT OF VEAL

If you are looking for a low-calorie dish to treat yourself – or some guests – then this is perfect, and quick, too.

INGREDIENTS

Serves 4
375g/12oz veal fillet or loin
10ml/2 tsp olive oil
10–12 tiny onions, kept whole
1 yellow pepper, seeded and cut
*   into eighths*
1 orange or red pepper, seeded and
*   cut into eighths*
3 tomatoes, peeled
*   and quartered*
4 fresh basil sprigs
30ml/2 tbsp dry martini or sherry
salt and black pepper

NUTRITION NOTES

Per portion:
Energy	158Kcals/665.5kJ
Fat	4.97g
Saturated Fat	1.14g
Cholesterol	63mg
Fibre	2.5g

1 Trim off any fat and cut the veal into cubes. Heat the oil in a frying pan and gently stir-fry the veal and onions until browned.

2 After a couple of minutes, add the peppers and tomatoes. Continue stir-frying for another 4–5 minutes.

COOK'S TIP
Lean beef or pork fillet may be used instead of veal, if you prefer. Shallots can replace the onions.

3 Add half the basil leaves, roughly chopped (keep some for garnish), the martini or sherry, and seasoning. Cook, stirring frequently, for another 10 minutes, or until the meat is tender.

4 Sprinkle with the remaining basil leaves and serve hot.

THAI BEEF SALAD

A hearty salad of beef, laced with a chilli and lime dressing.

INGREDIENTS

Serves 6

75g/3oz lean sirloin steaks
1 red onion, finely sliced
¹/₂ cucumber, finely sliced
*   into matchsticks*
1 lemon grass stalk, finely chopped
30ml/2 tbsp chopped spring onions
juice of 2 limes
15–30ml/1–2 tbsp fish sauce
2–4 red chillies, finely sliced, to garnish
fresh coriander, Chinese mustard cress
*   and mint leaves, to garnish*

NUTRITION NOTES

Per portion:	
Energy	101Kcals/424kJ
Fat	3.8g
Saturated Fat	1.7g
Cholesterol	33.4mg
Fibre	0.28g

COOK'S TIP
Rump or fillet steaks would work just as well in this recipe. Choose good-quality lean steaks and remove and discard any visible fat.

1 Grill the sirloin steaks until they are medium-rare, then allow to rest for 10–15 minutes.

2 When cool, thinly slice the beef and put the slices in a large bowl.

3 Add the sliced onion, cucumber matchsticks and lemon grass.

4 Add the spring onions. Toss and season with lime juice and fish sauce. Serve at room temperature or chilled, garnished with the chillies, coriander, mustard cress and mint.

THAI CHICKEN AND VEGETABLE STIR-FRY

Serves 4

1 piece lemon grass (or the rind of
 ½ lemon)
1cm/½in piece fresh root ginger
1 large garlic clove
30ml/2 tbsp sunflower oil
275g/10oz lean chicken,
 thinly sliced
½ red pepper, seeded and
 sliced
½ green pepper, seeded and sliced
4 spring onions, chopped
2 medium carrots, cut into matchsticks
115g/4oz fine green beans
25g/1oz peanuts, lightly crushed
30 ml/2 tbsp oyster sauce
pinch of sugar
salt and black pepper
coriander leaves, to garnish

NUTRITION NOTES

Per portion:

Energy	106Kcals/449kJ
Fat	2.05g
Saturated Fat	1.10g
Cholesterol	1.10mg
Fibre	109g

1 Thinly slice the lemon grass or lemon rind. Peel and chop the ginger and garlic. Heat the oil in a frying pan over a high heat. Add the lemon grass or lemon rind, ginger and garlic, and stir-fry for 30 seconds until brown.

2 Add the chicken and stir-fry for 2 minutes. Then add all the vegetables and stir-fry for 4–5 minutes, until the chicken is cooked and the vegetables are almost cooked.

3 Finally, stir in the peanuts, oyster sauce, sugar and seasoning to taste. Stir-fry for another minute to blend the flavours. Serve at once, sprinkled with the coriander leaves and accompanied by rice.

COOK'S TIP
Make this quick supper dish a little hotter by adding more fresh root ginger, if liked.

SPAGHETTI ALLA CARBONARA

This is a variation on the classic charcoal burner's spaghetti, using turkey rashers and low fat cream cheese instead of the traditional bacon and egg.

INGREDIENTS

Serves 4

150g/5oz smoked turkey rashers
oil, for frying
1 medium onion, chopped
1–2 garlic cloves, crushed
150ml/¼ pint/⅔ cup chicken stock
150ml/¼ pint/⅔ cup dry white wine
200g/7oz low fat cream cheese
450g/1lb chilli and garlic-flavoured
*   spaghetti*
30ml/2 tbsp chopped fresh parsley
salt and black pepper
shavings of Parmesan cheese,
*   to serve*

1 Cut the turkey rashers into 1cm/½in strips. Fry quickly in a non-stick pan for 2–3 minutes. Add the onion, garlic and stock to the pan. Bring to the boil, cover and simmer for about 5 minutes until tender.

2 Add the wine and boil rapidly until reduced by half. Whisk in the cream cheese and season to taste.

4 Return the spaghetti to the pan with the sauce and parsley, toss well and serve immediately with a few thin shavings of Parmesan cheese.

COOK'S TIP
If you can't find chilli and garlic-flavoured spaghetti, use plain spaghetti and add a small amount of raw chilli and garlic in step 4 or use the pasta of your choice.

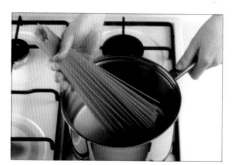

3 Meanwhile, cook the spaghetti in a large pan of boiling, salted water for 10–12 minutes until *al dente*. Drain thoroughly.

NUTRITION NOTES

Per portion:

Energy	500Kcals/2102kJ
Fat	3.3g
Saturated Fat	0.5g
Cholesterol	21mg
Fibre	4g

TURKEY AND PASTA BAKE

INGREDIENTS

Serves 4

275g/10oz minced turkey
150g/5oz smoked turkey rashers,
  chopped
1–2 garlic cloves, crushed
1 onion, finely chopped
2 carrots, diced
30ml/2 tbsp tomato purée
300ml/$^{1}/_{2}$ pint/1$^{1}/_{4}$ cups chicken stock
225g/8oz rigatoni or penne pasta
30ml/2 tbsp grated Parmesan cheese
salt and black pepper

1 Brown the minced turkey in a non-stick saucepan, breaking up any large pieces with a wooden spoon, until well browned all over.

2 Add the chopped turkey rashers, garlic, onion, carrots, purée, stock and seasoning. Bring to the boil, cover and simmer for 1 hour until tender.

3 Preheat the oven to 180°C/350°F/Gas 4. Cook the pasta in a large pan of boiling, salted water according to the packet instructions, until *al dente*. Drain thoroughly and mix with the turkey sauce.

COOK'S TIP
Minced chicken or extra lean minced beef work just as well in this tasty recipe.

4 Transfer to a shallow ovenproof dish and sprinkle with grated Parmesan cheese. Bake for 20–30 minutes until lightly browned on top.

NUTRITION NOTES	
Per portion:	
Energy	391Kcals/1641kJ
Fat	4.9g
Saturated Fat	2.2g
Cholesterol	60mg
Fibre	3.5g

TURKEY AND TOMATO HOT POT

Here, turkey is turned into tasty
meatballs in a rich tomato sauce.

INGREDIENTS

Serves 4

25g/1oz white bread, crusts removed
30ml/2 tbsp skimmed milk
1 garlic clove, crushed
2.5ml/½ tsp caraway seeds
225g/8oz minced turkey
1 egg white
350ml/12fl oz/1½ cups chicken stock
400g/14oz can tomatoes
15ml/1 tbsp tomato purée
90g/3½oz/½ cup easy-cook rice
salt and black pepper
fresh basil, to garnish
carrot and courgette ribbons, to serve

1 Cut the bread into small cubes and
put into a mixing bowl. Sprinkle
over the milk and leave to soak for
5 minutes.

2 Add the garlic clove, caraway seeds,
turkey and seasoning to the bread.
Mix together well.

3 Whisk the egg white until stiff, then
fold, half at a time, into the turkey
mixture. Chill for 10 minutes.

4 While the turkey mixture is chilling,
put the stock, tomatoes and tomato
purée into a large saucepan and bring
to the boil.

5 Add the rice, stir and cook briskly
for about 5 minutes. Turn the heat
down to a gentle simmer.

6 Meanwhile, shape the turkey
mixture into 16 small balls.
Carefully drop them into the tomato
stock and simmer for a further 8–10
minutes, or until both the turkey
balls and rice are cooked. Garnish
with basil, and serve with carrot and
courgette ribbons.

COOK'S TIPS
To make carrot and courgette
ribbons, cut the vegetables
lengthways into thin strips using
a vegetable peeler, and blanch or
steam until lightly cooked.

Lean minced turkey is low
in fat and is a good source of
protein. It makes an ideal base for
this tasty low fat supper dish. Use
minced chicken in place of turkey
for an appetizing alternative.

NUTRITION NOTES

Per portion:
Energy   190Kcals/798kJ
Protein   18.04g
Fat   1.88g
Saturated Fat   0.24g
Fibre   10.4g

Fish
and Seafood

CAJUN-STYLE COD

This recipe works equally well with any firm-fleshed fish – choose low fat fish, such as haddock or monkfish.

NUTRITION NOTES	
Per portion:	
Energy	137Kcals/577kJ
Protein	28.42g
Fat	1.75g
Saturated Fat	0.26g
Fibre	0.06g

INGREDIENTS

Serves 4

4 cod steaks, each weighing about
   175g/6oz
30ml/2 tbsp low fat natural yogurt
15ml/1 tbsp lime or lemon juice
1 garlic clove, crushed
5ml/1 tsp ground cumin
5ml/1 tsp paprika
5ml/1 tsp mustard powder
2.5ml/^{1}/2 tsp cayenne pepper
2.5ml/^{1}/2 tsp dried thyme
2.5ml/^{1}/2 tsp dried oregano
non-stick cooking spray
lemon slices, to garnish
new potatoes and a mixed salad,
   to serve

1 Pat the fish dry on kitchen paper. Mix together the yogurt and lime or lemon juice and brush lightly over both sides of the fish.

2 Mix together the crushed garlic, spices and herbs. Coat both sides of the fish with the seasoning mix, rubbing in well.

3 Spray a ridged grill pan or heavy-based frying pan with non-stick cooking spray. Heat until very hot. Add the fish and cook over a high heat for 4 minutes, or until the undersides are well browned.

4 Turn the steaks over and cook for a further 4 minutes, or until cooked through. Serve immediately, garnished with lemon and accompanied by new potatoes and a mixed salad.

PLAICE PROVENÇAL

Serves 4
4 large plaice fillets
2 small red onions
120ml/4fl oz/½ cup vegetable stock
60ml/4 tbsp dry red wine
1 garlic clove, crushed
2 courgettes, sliced
1 yellow pepper, seeded and sliced
400g/14oz can chopped tomatoes
15ml/1 tbsp chopped fresh thyme
salt and black pepper
potato gratin, to serve

1 Preheat the oven to 180°C/350°F/ Gas 4. Lay the plaice skin-side down and, holding the tail end, push a sharp knife between the skin and flesh in a sawing movement. Hold the knife at a slight angle with the blade towards the skin.

2 Cut each onion into eight wedges. Put into a heavy-based saucepan with the stock. Cover and simmer for 5 minutes. Uncover and continue to cook, stirring occasionally, until the stock has reduced entirely. Add the wine and garlic clove to the pan and continue to cook until the onions are soft.

3 Add the courgettes, yellow pepper, tomatoes and thyme and season to taste. Simmer for 3 minutes. Spoon the sauce into a large casserole.

COOK'S TIP
Skinless white fish fillets such as plaice are low in fat and make an ideal tasty and nutritious basis for many low fat recipes such as this one.

4 Fold each fillet in half and put on top of the sauce. Cover and cook in the oven for 15–20 minutes, until the fish is opaque and flakes easily. Serve with a potato gratin.

NUTRITION NOTES	
Per portion:	
Energy	191Kcals/802kJ
Protein	29.46g
Fat	3.77g
Saturated Fat	0.61g
Fibre	1.97g

MONKFISH AND MUSSEL SKEWERS

Skinless white fish such as monkfish is a good source of protein whilst also being low in calories and fat. These attractive seafood kebabs, flavoured with a light marinade, are excellent grilled or barbecued and served with herby boiled rice and a mixed leaf salad.

INGREDIENTS

Serves 4
450g/1lb monkfish, skinned and boned
5ml/1 tsp olive oil
30ml/2 tbsp lemon juice
5ml/1 tsp paprika
1 garlic clove, crushed
4 turkey rashers
8 cooked mussels
8 raw prawns
15ml/1 tbsp chopped fresh dill
salt and black pepper
lemon wedges, to garnish
salad leaves and long grain and wild
    rice, to serve

1 Cut the monkfish into 2.5cm/1in cubes and place in a shallow glass dish. Mix together the oil, lemon juice, paprika and garlic clove and season.

2 Pour the marinade over the fish and toss to coat evenly. Cover and leave in a cool place for 30 minutes.

3 Cut the turkey rashers in half and wrap each strip around a mussel. Thread on to skewers, alternating with the fish cubes and raw prawns. Preheat the grill to high.

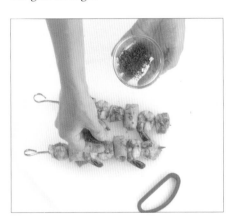

4 Grill the kebabs for 7–8 minutes, turning once and basting with the marinade. Sprinkle with chopped dill and salt. Garnish with lemon wedges and serve with salad and rice.

NUTRITION NOTES

Per portion:
Energy	133Kcals/560kJ
Protein	25.46g
Fat	3.23g
Saturated Fat	0.77g
Fibre	0.12g

LEMON SOLE BAKED IN A PAPER CASE

INGREDIENTS

Serves 4

4 lemon sole fillets, each weighing
  about 150g/5oz
1/2 small cucumber, sliced
4 lemon slices
60ml/4 tbsp dry white wine
sprigs of fresh dill, to garnish
potatoes and braised celery, to serve

For the yogurt hollandaise
150ml/1/4 pint low fat natural yogurt
5ml/1 tsp lemon juice
2 egg yolks
5ml/1 tsp Dijon mustard
salt and black pepper

1 Preheat the oven to 180°C/350°F/
Gas 4. Cut out four heart shapes
from non-stick baking paper, each
about 20 x 15cm/8 x 6in.

2 Place a sole fillet on one side of
each paper heart. Arrange the
cucumber and lemon slices on top of
each fillet. Sprinkle with the wine and
close the parcels by turning the edges of
the paper and twisting to secure. Put
on a baking tray and cook in the oven
for 15 minutes.

3 Meanwhile make the hollandaise.
Beat together the yogurt, lemon
juice and egg yolks in a double boiler
or bowl placed over a saucepan. Cook
over simmering water, stirring for
about 15 minutes, or until thickened.
(The sauce will become thinner after
10 minutes, but will thicken again.)

COOK'S TIP
Make sure that the paper parcels
are well sealed, so that none of
the delicious juices can escape.

4 Remove from the heat and stir in
the mustard. Season to taste with
salt and pepper. Open the fish parcels,
garnish with a sprig of dill and serve
accompanied with the sauce, new
potatoes and braised celery.

NUTRITION NOTES	
Per portion:	
Energy	185Kcals/779kJ
Protein	29.27g
Fat	4.99g
Saturated Fat	1.58g
Fibre	0.27g

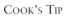

STEAMED FISH WITH CHILLI SAUCE

Steaming is one of the best – and lowest fat – methods of cooking fish. By leaving the fish whole and on the bone, you'll find that all the delicious flavour and moistness is retained.

INGREDIENTS

Serves 6

1 large or 2 medium, firm fish like bass or grouper, scaled and cleaned
a fresh banana leaf or large piece of foil
30ml/2 tbsp rice wine
3 red chillies, seeded and finely sliced
2 garlic cloves, finely chopped
2cm/³⁄₄in piece of fresh root ginger, finely shredded
2 lemon grass stalks, crushed and finely chopped
2 spring onions, chopped
30ml/2 tbsp fish sauce
juice of 1 lime

For the chilli sauce
10 red chillies, seeded and chopped
4 garlic cloves, chopped
60ml/4 tbsp fish sauce
15ml/1 tbsp sugar
75ml/5 tbsp lime juice

1 Rinse the fish under cold running water. Pat dry with kitchen paper. With a sharp knife, slash the skin of the fish a few times on both sides.

2 Place the fish on the banana leaf or foil. Mix together the remaining ingredients and spread over the fish.

3 Place a small upturned plate in the bottom of a wok or large frying pan, and add about 5cm/2in boiling water. Lay the banana leaf or foil with the fish on top on the plate and cover with a lid. Steam for about 10–15 minutes or until the fish is cooked.

4 Meanwhile, put all the chilli sauce ingredients in a food processor and process until smooth. You may need to add a little cold water.

5 Serve the fish hot, on the banana leaf if liked, with the sweet chilli sauce to spoon over the top.

NUTRITION NOTES	
Per portion:	
Energy	170Kcals/721kJ
Fat	3.46g
Saturated Fat	0.54g
Cholesterol	106mg
Fibre	0.35g

BAKED FISH IN BANANA LEAVES

Fish that is prepared in this way is particularly succulent and flavourful. Fillets are used here, rather than whole fish, which is easier for those who don't like to mess about with bones. It is a great dish for a barbecue.

INGREDIENTS

Serves 4
250ml/8fl oz/1 cup coconut milk
30ml/2 tbsp red curry paste
45ml/3 tbsp fish sauce
30ml/2 tbsp caster sugar
5 kaffir lime leaves, torn
4 x 175g/6oz fish fillets, such
  as snapper
175g/6oz mixed vegetables, such as
  carrots or leeks, finely shredded
4 banana leaves or pieces of foil
30ml/2 tbsp shredded spring onions, to
  garnish
2 red chillies, finely sliced, to garnish

NUTRITION NOTES

Per portion:	
Energy	258Kcals/1094kJ
Fat	4.31g
Saturated Fat	0.7g
Cholesterol	64.75mg
Fibre	1.23g

COOK'S TIP
Coconut milk is low in calories and fat and so makes an ideal basis for a low fat marinade or sauce. Choose colourful mixed vegetables such as carrots, leeks and red pepper, to make the dish more attractive and appealing.

1 Combine the coconut milk, curry paste, fish sauce, sugar and kaffir lime leaves in a shallow dish.

2 Marinate the fish in this mixture for about 15–30 minutes. Preheat the oven to 200°C/400°F/Gas 6.

3 Mix the vegetables together and lay a portion on top of a banana leaf or piece of foil. Place a piece of fish on top with a little of its marinade.

4 Wrap the fish up by turning in the sides and ends of the leaf and secure with cocktail sticks. (With foil, just crumple the edges together.) Repeat with the rest of the fish.

5 Bake for 20–25 minutes or until the fish is cooked. Alternatively, cook under the grill or on a barbecue. Just before serving, garnish the fish with a sprinkling of spring onions and sliced red chillies.

HERBY FISHCAKES WITH LEMON SAUCE

The wonderful flavour of fresh herbs makes these fishcakes the catch of the day.

INGREDIENTS

Serves 4

350g/12oz potatoes, roughly chopped
75ml/5 tbsp skimmed milk
350g/12oz haddock or hoki
 fillets, skinned
15ml/1 tbsp lemon juice
15ml/1 tbsp creamed horseradish sauce
30ml/2 tbsp chopped fresh parsley
flour, for dusting
115g/4oz/2 cups fresh wholemeal
 breadcrumbs
salt and black pepper
flat leaf parsley sprigs, to garnish
sugar snap peas or mange-tout and a
 sliced tomato and onion salad,
 to serve

For the lemon and chive sauce
thinly pared rind and juice of
 ½ small lemon
120ml/4fl oz/½ cup dry white wine
2 thin slices of fresh root ginger
10ml/2 tsp cornflour
30ml/2 tbsp snipped fresh chives

NUTRITION NOTES

Per portion:

Energy	232Kcals/975kJ
Protein	19.99g
Fat	1.99g
Saturated Fat	0.26g
Fibre	3.11g

COOK'S TIP
Dry white wine is a tasty fat-free basis for this herby sauce. Try using cider as an alternative to wine, for a change.

1 Cook the potatoes in a large saucepan of boiling water for 15–20 minutes. Drain and mash with the milk and season to taste.

2 Purée the fish together with the lemon juice and horseradish sauce in a blender or food processor. Mix with the potatoes and parsley.

3 With floured hands, shape the mixture into eight fishcakes and coat with the breadcrumbs. Chill in the fridge for 30 minutes.

4 Preheat the grill to medium and cook the fishcakes for 5 minutes on each side, until browned.

5 To make the sauce, cut the lemon rind into julienne strips and put into a large saucepan together with the lemon juice, wine and ginger. Season to taste with salt and pepper.

6 Simmer, uncovered, for about 6 minutes. Blend the cornflour with 15ml/1 tbsp of cold water, add to the pan and simmer until clear. Stir in the chives immediately before serving.

7 Serve the sauce hot with the fishcakes, garnished with parsley sprigs and accompanied with mange-tout and a tomato and onion salad.

MEDITERRANEAN FISH CUTLETS

These low fat fish cutlets are well complemented by boiled potatoes, broccoli and carrots.

INGREDIENTS

Serves 4

4 white fish cutlets, about 150g/5oz
each
about 150ml/¼ pint/⅔ cup fish stock
or dry white wine (or a mixture of
the two), for poaching
1 bay leaf, a few black peppercorns
and a strip of pared lemon rind, for
flavouring

For the tomato sauce
400g/14oz can chopped tomatoes
1 garlic clove, crushed
15ml/1 tbsp pastis or other aniseed-
flavoured liqueur
15ml/1 tbsp drained capers
12–16 stoned black olives
salt and black pepper

1 To make the sauce, place the chopped tomatoes, garlic, pastis or liqueur, capers and olives in a saucepan. Season to taste with salt and pepper and cook over a low heat for about 15 minutes, stirring occasionally.

2 Place the fish in a frying pan, pour over the stock and/or wine and add the bay leaf, peppercorns and lemon rind. Cover and simmer for 10 minutes or until it flakes easily.

3 Using a slotted spoon, transfer the fish into a heated dish. Strain the stock into the tomato sauce and boil to reduce slightly. Season the sauce, pour it over the fish and serve immediately, sprinkled with the chopped parsley.

COOK'S TIP
Remove skin from cutlets and reduce the quantity of olives to reduce calories and fat. Use 450g/1lb fresh tomatoes, skinned and chopped, in place of the canned tomatoes.

NUTRITION NOTES

Per portion:
Energy	165Kcals/685kJ
Fat	3.55g
Saturated Fat	0.5g
Cholesterol	69mg

BAKED COD WITH TOMATOES

For the very best flavour, use firm sun-ripened tomatoes for the sauce and make sure it is fairly thick before spooning it over the cod.

INGREDIENTS

Serves 4

10ml/2 tsp olive oil
1 onion, chopped
2 garlic cloves, finely chopped
450g/1lb tomatoes, peeled, seeded and chopped
5ml/1 tsp tomato purée
60ml/4 tbsp dry white wine
60ml/4 tbsp chopped flat leaf parsley
4 cod cutlets
30ml/2 tbsp dried breadcrumbs
salt and black pepper
new potatoes and green salad, to serve

NUTRITION NOTES

Per portion:

Energy	151Kcals/647kJ
Fat	1.5g
Saturated Fat	0.2g
Cholesterol	55.2mg
Fibre	2.42g

COOK'S TIP
For extra speed, use a 400g/14oz can of chopped tomatoes in place of the fresh tomatoes and 5–10ml/1–2 tsp ready-minced garlic in place of the garlic cloves.

1 Preheat the oven to 190°C/375°F/ Gas 5. Heat the oil in a pan and fry the onion for about 5 minutes. Add the garlic, tomatoes, tomato purée, wine and seasoning.

2 Bring the sauce just to the boil, then reduce the heat slightly and cook, uncovered, for 15–20 minutes until thick. Stir in the parsley.

3 Grease an ovenproof dish, put in the cod cutlets and spoon an equal quantity of the tomato sauce on to each. Sprinkle the dried breadcrumbs over the top.

4 Bake for 20–30 minutes, basting the fish occasionally with the sauce, until the fish is tender and cooked through, and the breadcrumbs are golden and crisp. Serve hot with new potatoes and a green salad.

Vegetable
Side Dishes

HERBY BAKED TOMATOES

INGREDIENTS

Serves 4–6

675g/1½ lb large red and yellow
  tomatoes
10ml/2 tsp red wine vinegar
2.5ml/½ tsp wholegrain mustard
1 garlic clove, crushed
10ml/2 tsp chopped fresh parsley
10ml/2 tsp snipped fresh chives
25g/1oz/½ cup fresh fine white
  breadcrumbs, for topping
salt and black pepper

NUTRITION NOTES

Per portion:
Energy	37Kcals/156kJ
Fat	0.49g
Saturated Fat	0.16g
Cholesterol	0
Fibre	1.36g

1 Preheat the oven to 200°C/400°F/
Gas 6. Thickly slice the tomatoes
and arrange half of them in a 900ml/
1½ pint/3¾ cup ovenproof dish.

COOK'S TIP
Use wholemeal breadcrumbs in
place of white, for added colour,
flavour and fibre. Use 5–10ml/
1–2 tsp mixed dried herbs, if fresh
herbs are not available.

2 Mix the vinegar, mustard, garlic
and seasoning together. Stir in
10ml/2 tsp cold water. Sprinkle the
tomatoes with half the parsley and
chives, then drizzle over half the
dressing.

3 Lay the remaining tomato slices on
top, overlapping them slightly.
Drizzle with the remaining dressing.

4 Sprinkle over the breadcrumbs.
Bake for 25 minutes or until the
topping is golden. Sprinkle with the
remaining parsley and chives. Serve
immediately, garnished with sprigs
of parsley.

POTATO GRATIN

The flavour of Parmesan is wonderfully strong, so a little goes a long way. Leave the cheese out altogether for an almost fat-free dish.

INGREDIENTS

Serves 4

1 garlic clove
5 large baking potatoes, peeled
45ml/3tbsp freshly grated Parmesan cheese
600ml/1 pint/2½ cups vegetable or chicken stock
pinch of grated nutmeg
salt and black pepper

1 Preheat the oven to 200°C/400°F/ Gas 6. Halve the garlic clove and rub over the base and sides of a large shallow gratin dish.

2 Slice the potatoes very thinly and arrange a third of them in the dish. Sprinkle with a little grated Parmesan cheese, and season with salt and pepper. Pour over some of the stock to prevent the potatoes from discolouring.

3 Continue layering the potatoes and cheese as before, then pour over the rest of the stock. Sprinkle with the grated nutmeg.

COOK'S TIP
For a potato and onion gratin, thinly slice one medium onion and layer with the potato.

4 Bake in the preheated oven for about 1¼–1½ hours or until the potatoes are tender and the tops well browned.

NUTRITION NOTES	
Per portion:	
Energy	178Kcals/749kJ
Protein	9.42g
Fat	1.57g
Saturated Fat	0.30g
Fibre	1.82g

CONCERTINA GARLIC POTATOES

With a low fat topping these would make a superb meal in themselves or could be enjoyed as a nutritious accompaniment to grilled fish or meat.

INGREDIENTS

Serves 4
4 baking potatoes
2 garlic cloves, cut into slivers
60ml/4 tbsp low fat fromage frais
60ml/4 tbsp low fat natural yogurt
30ml/2 tbsp snipped chives
6–8 watercress sprigs, finely chopped
(optional)

NUTRITION NOTES

Per portion:
Energy	195Kcals/815kJ
Fat	3.5g
Saturated Fat	2g
Cholesterol	10mg

1 Preheat the oven to 200°C/400°F/ Gas 6. Slice each potato at about 5mm/¼in intervals, cutting not quite to the base, so that they retain their shape. Slip the slivers of the garlic between the cuts in the potatoes.

COOK'S TIP
The most suitable potatoes for baking are of the floury variety. Some of the best include Estima, Cara and Kerr's Pink.

2 Place the garlic-filled potatoes in a roasting tin and bake for 1–1¼ hours or until soft when tested with a knife. Meanwhile, mix the low fat fromage frais and yogurt in a bowl, then stir in the snipped chives, along with the watercress, if using.

3 Serve the baked potatoes on individual plates, with a dollop of the yogurt and fromage frais mixture on top of each.

POTATO, LEEK AND TOMATO BAKE

INGREDIENTS

Serves 4
675g/1½lb potatoes
2 leeks, sliced
3 large tomatoes, sliced
a few fresh rosemary sprigs, crushed
1 garlic clove, crushed
300ml/½ pint/1¼ cups vegetable stock
15ml/1 tbsp olive oil
salt and black pepper

NUTRITION NOTES

Per portion:
Energy	180Kcals/740kJ
Fat	3.5g
Saturated Fat	0.5g
Cholesterol	0

1 Preheat the oven to 180°C/350°F/ Gas 4 and grease a 1.2 litre/ 2 pint/5 cup shallow ovenproof dish. Scrub and thinly slice the potatoes. Layer them with the leeks and tomatoes in the dish, scattering some rosemary between the layers and ending with a layer of potatoes.

2 Add the garlic to the stock, stir in salt if needed and pepper to taste, then pour over the vegetables. Brush the top layer of potatoes with olive oil.

3 Bake for 1¼–1½ hours until the potatoes are tender and the topping is golden and slightly crisp.

COURGETTES IN CITRUS SAUCE

If baby courgettes are unavailable, you can use larger ones, but they should be cooked whole so that they don't absorb too much water. After cooking, halve them lengthways and cut into 10cm/4in lengths. These tender, baby courgettes served in a very low fat sauce make this a tasty and low fat accompaniment to grilled fish fillets.

NUTRITION NOTES

Per portion:

Energy	33Kcals/138kJ
Protein	2.18g
Fat	0.42g
Saturated Fat	0.09g
Fibre	0.92g

INGREDIENTS

Serves 4

350g/12oz baby courgettes
4 spring onions, finely sliced
2.5cm/1in fresh root ginger, grated
30ml/2 tbsp cider vinegar
15ml/1 tbsp light soy sauce
5ml/1 tsp soft light brown sugar
45ml/3 tbsp vegetable stock
finely grated rind and juice of ½ lemon
*   and ½ orange*
5ml/1 tsp cornflour

1 Cook the courgettes in lightly salted boiling water for 3–4 minutes, or until just tender. Drain well.

2 Meanwhile, put all the remaining ingredients, except the cornflour, into a small saucepan and bring to the boil. Simmer for 3 minutes.

3 Blend the cornflour with 10ml/2 tsp cold water and add to the sauce. Bring to the boil, stirring continuously, until the sauce has thickened.

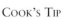

4 Pour the sauce over the courgettes and heat gently, shaking the pan to coat them evenly. Transfer to a warmed serving dish and serve.

COOK'S TIP
Use baby sweetcorn or aubergines in place of the courgettes for an appetizing change.

COURGETTE AND ASPARAGUS PARCELS

To appreciate the aroma, these paper parcels should be broken open at the table.

INGREDIENTS

Serves 4
2 medium courgettes
1 medium leek
225g/8oz young asparagus, trimmed
4 tarragon sprigs
4 whole garlic cloves, unpeeled
1 egg, beaten, to glaze
salt and black pepper

NUTRITION NOTES

Per portion:
Energy	110 Kcals/460kJ
Protein	6.22g
Fat	2.29g
Saturated Fat	0.49g
Fibre	6.73g

1 Preheat the oven to 200°C/400°F/ Gas 6. Using a potato peeler, carefully slice the courgettes lengthways into thin strips.

2 Cut the leek into very fine julienne strips and cut the asparagus evenly into 5cm/2in lengths.

3 Cut out four sheets of greaseproof paper measuring 30 x 38cm/ 12 x 15in and fold in half. Draw a large curve to make a heart shape when unfolded. Cut along the inside of the line and open out.

4 Divide the courgettes, asparagus and leek evenly between each paper heart, positioning the filling on one side of the fold line, and topping each with a sprig of tarragon and an unpeeled garlic clove. Season to taste.

5 Brush the edges lightly with the beaten egg and fold over.

6 Twist the edges together so that each parcel is completely sealed. Lay the parcels on a baking sheet and cook for 10 minutes. Serve immediately.

COOK'S TIP
Experiment with other vegetable combinations, if you like.

VEGETABLES À LA GRECQUE

This simple side salad is made with winter vegetables, but you can vary it according to the season. This combination of vegetables makes an ideal, low fat side salad to serve with grilled lean meat or poultry, or with thick slices of fresh, crusty bread.

INGREDIENTS

Serves 4

175ml/6fl oz/³⁄₄ cup white wine
5ml/1 tsp olive oil
30ml/2 tbsp lemon juice
2 bay leaves
sprig of fresh thyme
4 juniper berries
450g/1lb leeks, trimmed and cut into 2.5cm/1in lengths
1 small cauliflower, broken into florets
4 celery sticks, sliced on the diagonal
30ml/2 tbsp chopped fresh parsley
salt and black pepper

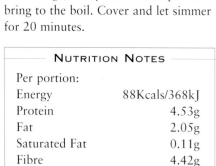

1 Put the wine, oil, lemon juice, bay leaves, thyme and juniper berries into a large, heavy-based saucepan and bring to the boil. Cover and let simmer for 20 minutes.

NUTRITION NOTES	
Per portion:	
Energy	88Kcals/368kJ
Protein	4.53g
Fat	2.05g
Saturated Fat	0.11g
Fibre	4.42g

2 Add the leeks, cauliflower and celery. Simmer very gently for 5–6 minutes or until just tender.

3 Remove the vegetables with a slotted spoon and transfer them to a serving dish. Briskly boil the cooking liquid for 15–20 minutes, or until reduced by half. Strain.

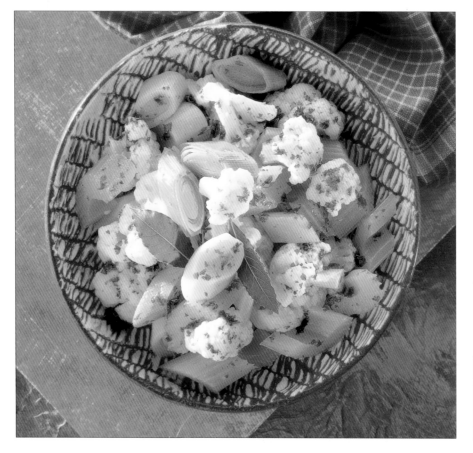

4 Stir the parsley into the liquid and season with salt and pepper to taste. Pour over the vegetables and leave to cool. Chill in the fridge for at least 1 hour before serving.

> COOK'S TIP
> Choose a dry or medium-dry white wine for best results.

ROASTED MEDITERRANEAN VEGETABLES

For a really colourful dish, try these vegetables roasted in olive oil with garlic and rosemary. The flavour is wonderfully intense.

INGREDIENTS

Serves 6
1 each red and yellow pepper
2 Spanish onions
2 large courgettes
1 large aubergine or 4 baby aubergines, trimmed
1 fennel bulb, thickly sliced
2 beef tomatoes
8 fat garlic cloves
30ml/2 tbsp olive oil
fresh rosemary sprigs
black pepper
lemon wedges and black olives (optional), to garnish

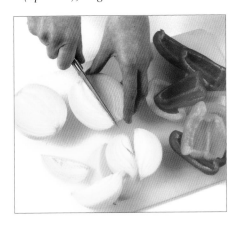

1 Halve and seed the peppers, then cut them into large chunks. Peel the onions and cut into thick wedges.

NUTRITION NOTES

Per portion:
Energy	120Kcals/504kJ
Fat	5.2g
Saturated Fat	0.68g
Cholesterol	0

2 Cut the courgettes and aubergines into large chunks.

3 Preheat the oven to 220°C/425°F/ Gas 7. Spread the peppers, onions, courgettes, aubergines and fennel in a lightly oiled, shallow ovenproof dish or roasting pan, or, if liked, arrange in rows to make a colourful design.

4 Cut each tomato in half and place, cut-side up, with the vegetables.

5 Tuck the garlic cloves among the vegetables, then brush them with the olive oil. Place some sprigs of rosemary among the vegetables and grind over some black pepper, particularly on the tomatoes.

6 Roast for 20–25 minutes, turning the vegetables halfway through the cooking time. Serve from the dish or on a flat platter, garnished with lemon wedges. Scatter some black olives over the top, if you like.

Desserts

Baked Apples in Honey and Lemon

A classic mix of flavours in a healthy, traditional family pudding. Serve warm, with skimmed-milk custard or low fat frozen yogurt.

Ingredients

Serves 4
4 medium cooking apples
15ml/1 tbsp clear honey
grated rind and juice of 1 lemon
15ml/1 tbsp low fat spread
skimmed-milk custard, to serve

1 Preheat the oven to 180°C/350°F/ Gas 4. Remove the cores from the apples, leaving them whole.

2 With a cannelle or sharp knife, cut lines through the apple skin at intervals. Put the apples in an oven-proof dish.

3 Mix together the honey, lemon rind, juice and low fat spread.

4 Spoon the mixture into the apples and cover the dish with foil or a lid. Bake for 40–45 minutes, or until the apples are tender. Serve with skimmed-milk custard.

APPLE AND BLACKCURRANT PANCAKES

These pancakes are made with a wholewheat batter and are filled with a delicious fruit mixture.

Makes 10
115g/4oz/1 cup plain wholemeal flour
300ml/½ pint/1¼ cups skimmed milk
1 egg, beaten
15ml/1 tbsp sunflower oil, plus extra
*   for greasing*
half fat crème fraîche, to serve
*   (optional)*
toasted nuts or sesame seeds, for
*   sprinkling (optional)*

For the filling
450g/1lb cooking apples
225g/8oz blackcurrants
30–45ml/2–3 tbsp water
30ml/2 tbsp demerara sugar

1 To make the pancake batter, put the flour in a mixing bowl and make a well in the centre.

2 Add a little of the milk with the egg and the oil. Beat the flour into the liquid, then gradually beat in the rest of the milk, keeping the batter smooth and free from lumps. Cover the batter and chill while you prepare the filling.

> COOK'S TIP
> If you wish, substitute other combinations of fruit for apples and blackcurrants.

3 Quarter, peel and core the apples. Slice them into a pan and add the blackcurrants and water. Cook over a gentle heat for 10–15 minutes until the fruit is soft. Stir in enough demerara sugar to sweeten.

NUTRITION NOTES	
Per portion:	
Energy	120Kcals/505kJ
Fat	3g
Saturated Fat	0.5g
Cholesterol	25mg

4 Lightly grease a non-stick pan with just a smear of oil. Heat the pan, pour in about 30ml/2 tbsp of the batter, swirl it around and cook for about 1 minute. Flip the pancake over with a palette knife and cook the other side. Put on a sheet of kitchen paper and keep hot while cooking the remaining pancakes.

5 Fill the pancakes with the apple and blackcurrant mixture and roll them up. Serve with a dollop of crème fraîche, if using, and sprinkle with nuts or sesame seeds, if liked.

CINNAMON AND APRICOT SOUFFLÉS

Don't expect these to be difficult simply because they're soufflés – they really couldn't be easier, and, best of all, they're very low in calories.

INGREDIENTS

Serves 4
3 eggs
115g/4oz/½ cup apricot fruit spread
finely grated rind of ½ lemon
5ml/1 tsp ground cinnamon
extra cinnamon, to decorate

NUTRITION NOTES

Per portion:
Energy	102Kcals/429kJ
Fat	4.97g
Saturated Fat	1.42g
Cholesterol	176.25mg
Fibre	0

1 Preheat the oven to 190°C/375°F/ Gas 5. Lightly grease four individual soufflé dishes and dust them lightly with flour.

2 Separate the eggs and put the yolks in a bowl with the fruit spread, lemon rind and cinnamon.

3 Whisk hard until the mixture is thick and pale in colour.

4 Place the egg whites in a clean bowl and whisk them until they are stiff enough to hold soft peaks.

5 Using a large metal spoon or spatula, fold the egg whites evenly into the yolk mixture.

6 Divide the soufflé mixture between the prepared dishes and bake for 10–15 minutes, until well risen and golden brown. Serve immediately, dusted with a little extra cinnamon.

COOK'S TIP
Puréed fresh or well-drained canned fruit can be used instead of the apricot spread, but make sure the mixture is not too wet, or the soufflés will not rise properly.

BLUEBERRY AND ORANGE CRÊPE BASKETS

Impress your guests with these pretty, fruit-filled crêpes. When blueberries are out of season, replace them with other soft fruit, such as raspberries.

INGREDIENTS

Serves 6
150g/5oz/1¼ cups plain flour
pinch of salt
2 egg whites
200ml/7fl oz/⅞ cup skimmed milk
150ml/¼ pint/⅔ cup orange juice
oil, for frying
yogurt or light crème fraîche, to serve

For the filling
4 medium oranges
225g/8oz/2 cups blueberries

1 Preheat the oven to 200°C/400°F/ Gas 6. To make the pancakes, sift the flour and salt into a bowl. Make a well in the centre and add the egg whites, milk and orange juice. Whisk hard, until all the liquid has been incorporated and the batter is smooth and bubbly.

2 Lightly grease a heavy or non-stick pancake pan and heat it until it is very hot. Pour in just enough batter to cover the base of the pan, swirling it to cover the pan evenly.

3 Cook until the pancake has set and is golden, then turn it to cook the other side. Remove the pancake to a sheet of kitchen paper. Cook the remaining batter to make 6–8 pancakes.

4 Place six small ovenproof bowls or moulds on a baking sheet and lay the pancakes over these. Bake them in the oven for about 10 minutes, until they are crisp and set into shape. Lift the 'baskets' off the moulds.

5 Pare a thin piece of orange rind from one orange and cut it into fine strips. Blanch the strips in boiling water for 30 seconds, rinse them in cold water and set them aside. Cut all the peel and white pith from the oranges.

6 Divide the oranges into segments, catching the juice, combine with the blueberries and warm them gently. Spoon the fruit into the baskets and scatter the rind over the top. Serve with yogurt or light crème fraîche.

COOK'S TIP
Don't fill the pancake baskets until you're ready to serve them, because they will absorb the fruit juice and begin to soften.

NUTRITION NOTES

Per portion:

Energy	157.3Kcals/668.3kJ
Fat	2.20g
Saturated Fat	0.23g
Cholesterol	0.66mg
Fibre	2.87g

FILO CHIFFON PIE

Filo pastry is low in fat and is very easy to use. Keep a pack in the freezer, ready to make impressive desserts like this one.

INGREDIENTS

Serves 6
500g/1¼lb rhubarb
5ml/1 tsp mixed spice
finely grated rind and juice of 1 orange
15ml/1 tbsp granulated sugar
15g/½oz/1 tbsp butter
3 filo pastry sheets

1 Preheat the oven to 200°C/400°F/ Gas 6. Chop the rhubarb into 2.5cm/1in pieces and put them in a bowl.

2 Add the mixed spice, orange rind and juice and sugar. Tip the rhubarb into a 1 litre/1¾ pint/4 cup pie dish.

NUTRITION NOTES

Per portion:
Energy	71Kcals/299kJ
Fat	2.5g
Saturated Fat	1.41g
Cholesterol	5.74mg
Fibre	1.48g

3 Melt the butter and brush it over the pastry. Lift the pastry on to the pie dish, butter-side up, and crumple it up decoratively to cover the pie.

VARIATION
Other fruit can be used in this pie – just prepare depending on type.

4 Put the dish on a baking sheet and bake for 20 minutes, until golden brown. Reduce the heat to 180°C/350°F/ Gas 4 and bake for a further 10–15 minutes, until the rhubarb is tender.

CRUNCHY FRUIT LAYER

INGREDIENTS

Serves 2

1 peach or nectarine
75g/3oz/1 cup crunchy toasted
* oat cereal*
150ml/¼ pint/⅔ cup low fat
* natural yogurt*
15ml/1 tbsp jam
15ml/1 tbsp fruit juice

NUTRITION NOTES

Per portion:
Energy	240Kcals/1005kJ
Fat	3g
Saturated Fat	1g
Cholesterol	3mg

1 Remove the stone from the peach or nectarine and cut the fruit into bite-size pieces with a sharp knife.

2 Divide the chopped fruit between two tall glasses, reserving a few pieces for decoration.

3 Sprinkle the oat cereal over the fruit in an even layer, then top with the low fat yogurt.

4 Stir the jam and the fruit juice together in a jug, then drizzle the mixture over the yogurt. Decorate with the reserved peach or nectarine pieces and serve at once.

ICED ORANGES

The ultimate fat-free treat –
these delectable orange sorbets
served in fruit shells were origi-
nally sold in the beach cafés in
the south of France.

INGREDIENTS

Serves 8

150g/5oz/⅔ cup granulated sugar
juice of 1 lemon
14 medium oranges
8 fresh bay leaves, to decorate

NUTRITION NOTES

Per portion:	
Energy	139Kcals/593kJ
Fat	0.17g
Saturated Fat	0
Cholesterol	0
Fibre	3g

COOK'S TIP
Use crumpled kitchen paper to
keep the shells upright.

1 Put the sugar in a heavy-based
saucepan. Add half the lemon juice,
then add 120ml/4fl oz/½ cup water.
Cook over a low heat until the sugar
has dissolved. Bring to the boil and boil
for 2–3 minutes until the syrup is clear.

2 Slice the tops off eight of the
oranges to make "hats". Scoop out
the flesh of the oranges and reserve.
Freeze the empty orange shells and
"hats" until needed.

3 Grate the rind of the remaining
oranges and add to the syrup.
Squeeze the juice from the oranges, and
from the reserved flesh. There should
be 750ml/1¼ pints/3 cups. Squeeze
another orange or add bought orange
juice, if necessary.

4 Stir the orange juice and remaining
lemon juice, with 90ml/6 tbsp water
into the syrup. Taste, adding more
lemon juice or sugar as desired. Pour
the mixture into a shallow freezer
container and freeze for 3 hours.

5 Turn the orange sorbet mixture into
a bowl and whisk thoroughly to
break up the ice crystals. Freeze for
4 hours more, until firm, but not solid.

6 Pack the mixture into the hollowed-
out orange shells, mounding it up,
and set the "hats" on top. Freeze the
sorbet shells until ready to serve. Just
before serving, push a skewer into the
tops of the "hats" and push in a bay
leaf, to decorate.

RASPBERRY VACHERIN

Meringue rounds filled with orange-flavoured low fat fromage frais and fresh raspberries make this a perfect dinner party dessert.

INGREDIENTS

Serves 6
3 egg whites
175g/6oz/³/4 cup caster sugar
5ml/1 tsp chopped almonds
icing sugar, for dusting
raspberry leaves, to decorate (optional)

For the filling
175g/6oz/³/4 cup low fat soft cheese
15–30ml/1–2 tbsp clear honey
15–30ml/1–2 tbsp Cointreau
120ml/4fl oz/¹/2 cup low fat
    fromage frais
225g/8oz raspberries

NUTRITION NOTES

Per portion:
Energy	197Kcals/837.5kJ
Fat	1.02g
Saturated Fat	0.36g
Cholesterol	1.67mg
Fibre	1g

COOK'S TIP
When making the meringue, whisk the egg whites until they are so stiff that you can turn the bowl upside-down without them falling out.

1 Preheat the oven to 140°C/275°F/ Gas 1. Draw a 20cm/8in circle on two pieces of non-stick baking paper. Turn the paper over so the marking is on the underside and use it to line two heavy baking sheets.

2 Whisk the egg whites in a clean bowl until very stiff, then gradually whisk in the caster sugar to make a stiff meringue mixture.

3 Spoon the mixture on to the circles on the prepared baking sheets, spreading the meringue evenly to the edges. Sprinkle one meringue round with the chopped almonds.

4 Bake for 1¹/2–2 hours until crisp and dry, and then carefully lift the meringue rounds off the baking sheets. Peel away the paper and cool the meringues on a wire rack.

5 To make the filling, cream the soft cheese with the honey and liqueur in a bowl. Gradually fold in the fromage frais and the raspberries, reserving three berries for decoration.

6 Place the plain meringue round on a board, spread with the filling and top with the nut-covered round. Dust with the icing sugar, transfer to a serving plate and decorate with the reserved raspberries and a sprig of raspberry leaves, if you like.

TROPICAL FOAMY YOGURT RING

An impressive, light and colourful tropical dessert with a truly fruity flavour.

INGREDIENTS

Serves 6
For the yogurt ring
175ml/6fl oz/³⁄₄ cup tropical fruit juice
15ml/1 tbsp/1 sachet powdered gelatine
3 egg whites
150g/5oz low fat natural yogurt
finely grated rind of 1 lime

For the filling
1 mango
2 kiwi fruit
10–12 physalis cape gooseberries
juice of 1 lime

1 Place the tropical fruit juice in a small pan and sprinkle the powdered gelatine over. Heat gently until the gelatine has dissolved.

2 Whisk the egg whites in a clean, dry bowl until they hold soft peaks. Continue whisking hard, while gradually adding the yogurt and lime rind.

3 Continue whisking hard and pour in the hot gelatine and the egg white and yogurt mixture in a steady stream, until everything is smooth and evenly mixed.

4 Quickly pour the mixture into a 1.5 litre/2½ pint/6¼ cup ring mould. Chill the mould in the fridge until set. The mixture will separate into two layers.

5 Halve, stone, peel and dice the mango. Peel and slice the kiwi fruit. Remove the outer leaves from the physalis and cut in half. Toss all the fruits together and stir in the lime juice.

6 Run a knife around the edge of the ring to loosen the mixture. Dip the tin quickly into cold water and then turn the chilled yogurt mould out on to a serving plate. Spoon all the prepared fruit into the centre of the ring and serve immediately.

NUTRITION NOTES

Per portion:	
Energy	83.5Kcals/355kJ
Fat	0.67g
Saturated Fat	0.27g
Cholesterol	2.16mg
Fibre	1.77g

COOK'S TIP
Any mixture of fruit works in this recipe, depending on the season. In summer try using apple juice in the ring mixture and fill it with luscious, red summer fruits.

Index